THE COWBOY'S COOKBOOK

Also by Sherry Monahan

Frontier Fare: Recipes and Lore from the Old West

Mrs. Earp: The Wives and Lovers of the Earp Brothers

THE COWBOY'S COOKBOOK

Recipes and Tales from Campfires, Cookouts, and Chuck Wagons

SHERRY MONAHAN

TWODOT®

GUILFORD, CONNECTICUT
HELENA, MONTANA

A · TWODOT® · BOOK

An imprint and registered trademark of Rowman & Littlefield

Distributed by NATIONAL BOOK NETWORK

British Library Cataloguing-in-Publication Information available

Library of Congress Cataloging-in-Publication Data

Monahan, Sherry.
  The cowboy's cookbook : recipes and tales from campfires, cookouts, and chuck wagons / Sherry Monahan.
     pages cm
  Includes bibliographical references and index.
  ISBN 978-1-4930-1067-7 (pbk. : alk. paper) — ISBN 978-1-4930-1610-5 (e-book)
1. Cooking, American—Western style. 2. Cowboys—West (U.S.) 3. Cooking, American—Southwestern style. 4. Cowboys—Southwest, New. I. Title.
  TX715.2.W47M655 2015
  641.5978—dc23

                                                                                    2015017394

∞™ The paper used in this publication meets the minimum requirements of American National Standard for Information Sciences—Permanence of Paper for Printed Library Materials, ANSI/NISO Z39.48-1992.

CONTENTS

ACKNOWLEDGMENTS

Thanks to Erin Turner at TwoDot/Globe Pequot for asking me to create this fun book. Special thanks to all those who shared recipes, photos, and stories: Steve Turner, Gail Jenner, and Kellen Cutsforth. Thanks also to the daring souls who volunteered to test some of these nineteenth-century recipes for me: Micki Fuhrman Milom, Rod Timanus, Jennifer Faircloth, Bev and Dave MacBrien, and Lyndsay Fogarty. Also thanks to my husband for eating many of the results of these recipes!

INTRODUCTION

Sop, lick, sinkers, and whistle berries. Those all sound tasty, don't they? Well, the cowboys had a language all their own when it came to many things. Now, they really aren't as bad as they sound. Sop was nothing more than gravy. Lick was molasses or some other kind of syrup. Sinkers were biscuits. And whistle berries, well, they were beans, and you can probably guess why they were called whistle berries.

Even the term *cowboy* had different meanings. It has been defined in many ways by many people over the years. I did a little research and found that in the 1860s it was more of a derogatory term than a description. An editorial in the 1869 *Leavenworth Bulletin* of Kansas included this statement: "*The Atchison Champion & Press* flies at the *Bulletin* in a terrible rage and with the manners of a cow-boy . . ."

Even though the term was being used at that time, it did not appear in *Webster's Complete Dictionary of the English Language* until 1884. The entry did not describe the western cowboy, however; it referred to a marauder from the Revolutionary War era. That soon changed, and *cowboy* came to describe someone who worked with or watched cattle.

By 1895 the big cattle drives were over and a new definition for the word *cowboy* appeared in *Webster's Collegiate Dictionary: A Dictionary of the English Language*. The definition was: "a cattle herder; a drover." By 1913 the definition was expanded: "A cattle herder, esp. one of a class of mounted herdsmen of the western United States." The cowboys themselves often called each other *waddies*, which was interchangeable with *cowhand* or *cowpuncher*.

When describing the cowboy, noted historian and award-winning author Robert Utley says it best. In his book, *Encyclopedia of the American West*, he writes, "No figure more vividly personifies the Old West than the cowboy—the plainsman who tended cattle during the heyday of the open range." The cattle drives lasted in earnest for about twenty years between 1866 and 1886. When the open ranges began to be fenced in with barbed wire in the late 1880s to prevent overgrazing, the cattle drives began to trail off.

Even though most cowboys loved sleeping under the stars and working with the cattle, they had a tough life. They earned about forty dollars per month. Not all cowboys working for a ranch rode horses during roundups or trail drives. Many started their work on a ranch by mending fences, cleaning stables, removing cows from bogs, and doing other miscellaneous tasks. Most worked their way up the ranks if they weren't skilled horsemen. According to Agnes Morley Cleaveland, who was raised on a New Mexico ranch and later ran it, "The ascending scale in open-range business is from horse wrangler at the lowest rung to range boss at the highest. Between them lie cook, riders, fence-line riders (after there were fences), and run-of-the-mill waddies."

J. T. "Sad" Gardenhire was one of those men and he recalled, "I am Sad Gardenhire and I used to be a cow puncher when a man had to be a cow puncher and not just a range hand. Doing everything from slopping hogs to farming. Not only that, but he had to ride the first hoss he come to and couldn't be choicy. And, that was in a day when nigh unto every hoss was about half outlaw. Now, that all sounds pretty bad but when you're used to anything, it ain't so bad. That's the kind of life we were used to, so that's the kind of a life we lived. Rough and tough with a lot of hard work throwed in for good measure."

Once cowboys got horse work, they rode on the spring and fall roundups, which could last up to six weeks. On the trail for months at a time, they often endured extreme weather and a variety of other hardships. Some trekked up and down trails, including the famous Chisolm Trail, while herding the cattle until they arrived at their destination.

Cowboys and cattle drives weren't just limited to Texas and Kansas, although the drives were most numerous in those states. Cattle ranches dotted the western frontier like a cowhide tapestry. Large cattle ranches could be found in Wyoming, Montana, Nebraska, Arizona Territory, Colorado, the Dakota Territory, Oregon, and California. While they didn't travel the well-known Chisholm Trail, they did move, corral, and brand their cattle just the same. Regardless of where the ranches were, their goal was to get their cattle to a railroad so the animals could be shipped for processing. Ranches like those deep in Texas drove their cattle to large railheads while other in Montana or Wyoming were near the train lines.

The chuck wagon and its cook were the lifeblood of the cowboy during roundups and while on the trail. Sometimes the cooks were really good; sometimes they just got by with providing the basics. But the bad cooks were harassed by the cowboys and didn't tend to last too long. Most ranch owners wanted their cowboys fed well so that they would stay healthy and happy along the trail. The *cookie*, as he was often referred to, made all their meals, mended their clothes, provided health care, and often acted as their caretaker or parent.

After the spring round up, the cowboys and their cattle headed out on the trail. Their final destination would be a cow town that had a railroad station where the cattle was corralled and eventually loaded for the market. When the cowboys got to a cow town, their job was done and they were paid. They got washed, wild, and womanized for a few days.

Once they finished "celebrating" in town, they headed home. Sometimes the cowboys would head back to their ranch with the chuck wagon cook or with other cowboys. While at the ranch they handled daily chores that included branding, wrangling, mending, and anything else that needed attention. Their bunkhouse was meager, but it provided them with beds, a roof over their heads, and meals.

It was often up to the cowboys themselves to cook in the bunkhouse, but the cookie did live there, too. Those who lived on small ranches often took their meals with the family in the main house. Cowboys living on the bigger ranches were sometimes invited to the big house, that is, the boss's house for meals on special occasions like Christmas.

This cast-iron saucepan and coffeepot are from the 1880s and would have been used on cattle drives, roundups, or in ranch houses.

This collection of stories and recipes will let you peek into the lives of the men, and, on rare occasions, women, who were called cowboys. Read about them from their firsthand accounts, those of the trail bosses, and those of the townspeople they sometimes offended. Sources include the Library of Congress' American Memory Project and nineteenth-century publications. The recipes come from many sources, including longtime ranch families, historic restaurants, and local papers of the day. Not all recipes are from the places mentioned in stories, but are typical of the time period in the American West.

I hope that after reading this you get a sense of the identity of the American cowboy and cattleman, his rugged life, and the food that got him through it all.

Cheers!

COOKING NOTES

Using nineteenth-century recipes can be tricky. Cooking terminology, ingredients, and techniques vary from what we know today. I've created some notes to help with these recipes.

These are authentic recipes from nineteenth-century newspapers, families, and cookbooks west of the Mississippi, except for *Camping and Camp Cooking*, which was printed in Boston. Although it was published in the East, it could have easily been used in the West. I used it because many of the techniques used on the cattle trails and round-ups amounted to those used in camping and outdoor cooking.

Here is a list of "Household Hints" for cooking. That term was used to alert cooks reading the newspapers that the topics below the headline had to do with cooking.

- Never pack down flour in a measuring cup unless specifically told to do so.

- Always allow cooked meat to rest for five to ten minutes before cutting so the juices will stay in the meat and not on the plate.

- You can create your own buttermilk by adding 1 teaspoon of white vinegar to 1 cup of milk.

- Bread flour is best for baking bread because of its higher gluten content.

- When using dried fruits like raisins, soak them in a small amount of liquid to rehydrate before cooking with them.

- Freshly ground pepper tastes much better than pre-ground.

- Substitute 1 teaspoon of dried herbs for 3 tablespoons of fresh.

- Make dressing ahead and chill so a hot mixture isn't being stuffed into a bird.

DUTCH OVEN COOKING

Here are cooking tips for those wanting to prepare food like the cookies on the trail.

- Start with a well-seasoned cast iron oven or pan. Please note that cooking with a dutch oven takes practice and while the following are basic guidelines, they may need to be adjusted depending upon the altitude, temperature, and wind.

- You can bake directly in the dutch oven or place the food in a baking pan and set the pan in the dutch oven.

- The number of coals used is tied to the size of the dutch oven itself. The temperature needed to cook also matters. So to bake something at 350°F in a 12-inch oven, twenty-four briquettes in total are needed. When baking place eighteen on the top and six underneath. The basic formula when baking is to use twice the number of briquettes as the diameter of the oven with three-quarters of them on the lid.

- When frying or boiling, place all the coals underneath. For simmering, place three-quarters of them under the oven and one-quarter on top.

- Most coals should last between 30 and 45 minutes, so additional coals might be needed if cooking time is longer. Have additional coals ready to go on or under the oven when needed.

The dutch oven was not only used to cook stews. Often, for example, a bread pan would be filled and placed into the dutch oven. It was covered and placed on hot coals, and more coals were placed on top of it. Thus it became an appliance-type oven for baking breads and cakes.

When adding coals remember that, on average, each briquette produces about 10°–15°F worth of heat on a moderately warm day with no wind.

- Wind causes the briquettes to burn faster; if possible, try to dig a hole to protect the coals during cooking. Outdoor temperatures also impact cooking times. Food will cook quicker when it's hot outside and slower when it's colder.

- Arrange the coals in a circle under the oven and evenly cover the top or place the briquettes in a checkerboard pattern for even heat distribution.

Number of Briquettes to Reach Desired Temperature When Baking

Temp.	8"	8"	10"	10"	12"	12"	14"	14"	16"	16"
°F	Over	Under	Over	Under	Over	Under	Over	Under	Over	Under
300°	9	3	12	4	15	5	18	6	21	7
325°	10	3	14	4	17	5	20	6	23	7
350°	11	5	13	7	16	8	21	7	24	8
375°	14	4	17	5	20	6	23	7	26	8
400°	15	5	18	6	21	7	24	8	27	9
425°	17	5	20	6	23	7	26	8	29	9
450°	18	6	21	7	24	8	27	9	30	10

Source: Byron's Dutch Oven Cooking, http://papadutch.home.comcast.net/~papadutch/

COWBOY VERNACULAR

Author and researcher Ramon F. Adams spent years interviewing cowboys and cataloging their vocabulary. The following is a list of food terms and their definitions from his 1944 book, *Western Words: A Dictionary of the Range, Cow Camp and Trail* (University of Oklahoma Press).

Chuck-box: It was bolted to the rear of the chuck wagon with a hinged lid that, when let down and supported by a stout leg, forms a wide shelf or table. This is the cook's private property and woe unto the nervy puncher who tries to use it for a dining table. Occasionally this privilege is granted to the wrangler, who generally eats after all the others have finished and are changing horses, but never to a rider.

Cook: Bean-master, belly cheater, biscuit roller, biscuit shooter, cocinero, cookie, cook's louse, coosie, dinero, dough-belly, dough-boxer, dough-puncher, dough roller, dough-wrangler, flunky, greasy belly, grub spoiler, grub worm, gut robber, old woman, pothooks, pot rustler, Sallie, sheffi, sop an' 'taters, sourdough, and swamper.

Cook Shack: The kitchen, especially when a separate building.

Cook's Implements: Dutch oven, flunky, gouch hook, lizard scorcher, pothook, round pan, squirrel can, swamper, wreck pan.

Coosie: Borrowing from the Spanish, the Southwest cow country called the cook cocinero, and from this came the common nickname coosie.

Cowboy: This word seems to have originated in Revolutionary days . . . The next men we find calling themselves by this name are a bunch of wild-riding, reckless Texans under the leadership of Ewen Cameron, who spent their time chasing longhorns and Mexicans soon after Texas became a republic . . . Then came the real cowboy as we know him today—a man who followed the cows. He has been called everything from a cow poke to a dude wrangler, but never a coward. He is still with us today and will always be as long as the West raises cows, changing, perhaps, with the times, but always witty, friendly, and fearless.

Cow Chips: Dried cow or buffalo droppings: A popular fuel in the early days on the plains, where timber was scarce. It was hard to get a fire started with them, but when dry, this "prairie coal" made a hot one.

Cow Grease: A slang name for butter.

Crumb Castle: A slang name for the chuck wagon.

Cutting the Herd: Inspecting a trail herd for cattle which do not properly belong in it.

Dive/Dump: Slang names for the bunkhouse.

Dough Gods: A slang name for biscuits.

Dutch Oven: A very thick, three-footed skillet with a heavy lid. It is used for cooking much of the cowboy's food, but especially biscuits. It is placed over hot coals with more coals put on the lid, thus browning the food on both sides.

Feed Trough: Another slang name for the eating house.

Fly: A sheet which is stretched at the end of the chuck wagon to make shade and shelter for the cook.

Fried Chicken: A sarcastic name for bacon which has been rolled in flour and fried.

Gouch-hook: A pot-hook used by the cook for lifting the heavy lids of his cooking utensils.

Greasy-sack outfit: A small ranch outfit which carries its commissary pack in a sack on a mule in lieu of a chuck wagon.

Growler: A slang name for the chuck wagon.

Grub house: A slang name for the cook shack.

Grub-pile: A meal; often the call to meals.

Gut shrunk: Having been without food for a considerable time.

Hacienda: A Spanish noun meaning a landed estate, usually the homestead of the owner, devoted to stock raising.

Heel squatter: The cowboy is sometimes called thus because it is a common practice for him to rest by squatting upon his heels. This is not a comfortable seat for the layman, but the cowboy will squat comfortably on his boot-heels to eat his meals when out on the range, to spin his yarns, and, in fact, he is always ready "to take comfort in a frog squat."

Honkytonk town: The towns at the end of the old cattle trails came under this classification, as their business districts were composed largely of saloons and honkytonks. Such towns were tough and, as the cowman would say, a "bad place to have your gun stick."

Huckydummy: Baking powder bread with raisins.

Immigrant butter: Gravy made from bacon grease, flour, and water.

Indian bread: This was a tasty strip of fatty matter starting from the shoulder blade and extending backward along the backbone of a buffalo. When scalded in hot grease to seal it, then smoked, it became a tidbit the buffalo hunter used as bread. When eaten with lean or dried meat it made an excellent sandwich.

Jamoka: An occasional name for coffee made by combining Java and Mocha.

Jerky: Dried beef. From the Mexican Indian word *charqui* (char'kee). The Spanish and the Indians first dried buffalo meat by cutting it thin and drying it in the sun. When dry, it could be ground up like meal. When cooked in a soup, it swelled to considerable proportions and served as a nourishing food. Later the white man followed their example, and jerky became a staple food.

John Chinaman: What the cowboy calls boiled rice.

Kansas City fish: Fried salt pork.

Lick: The cowboy's name for molasses.

Lining his flue: Said of one eating.

Lizard scorcher: A camp stove.

Long sweetenin': Slang name for molasses.

Machinery belting: Tough beef.

Man at the pot: If a man in camp, during meals, gets up to refill his cup with coffee and this is yelled at him, he is duty-bound by camp etiquette to go around with the pot and fill all the cups that are held out to him.

Mess house: The cook shack.

Mess wagon: Another name for the chuck wagon.

Mexican strawberries: A slang name for dried beans.

Mountain oyster: A testicle of a bull. Some find it a choice delicacy when roasted or fried.

Moving camp: When a roundup camp is to be moved, the wagon boss gives instructions which no one but a cowhand familiar with the country could understand. Every cowhand finds something to do, or he is not a cowboy. Some harness the cook's teams while others help him pack and stow his pots and utensils . . . The mess wagon is rattling and swaying behind that running team until he wonders how the outfit holds together. By the time the cowboys reach the new camp at noon, the cook will have camp set up and a hot meal waiting for them.

Old woman: Affectionate name for the cook, but said behind his back.

Pie-biter: A horse which secretly forages the camp kitchen to indulge his acquired tastes.

Pie-box: A slang name for the chuck wagon, perhaps in wishful thinking.

Pie wagon: A trailer used behind the chuck wagon.

Pooch: The name of a dish made of tomatoes, sugar, and bread.

Potluck: As used by the cowman and other frontiersmen, this means food contributed by a guest. To bring potluck is to bring food with one.

Ram pasture: An occasional name for the bunkhouse.

Sinkers: Slang name for biscuits.

Skid grease: Slang name for butter.

Slow elk: To kill for food an animal belonging to someone else (as verb); beef butchered without the owner's knowledge (as noun). Some cowmen followed the philosophy that "One's own beef don't taste as good as the other feller's because fat, tender yearling's what you kill when they're other folk's stuff."

Son of a B Stew: A favorite dish of the cowboy made of the brains, sweetbreads, and choice pieces of a freshly killed calf. If the cowhand wishes to be polite he calls it son-of-a-gun, but if no delicate ears are present, he calls it by its true fighting name. When a calf is killed, the tongue, liver, heart, kidneys, sweetbreads, and brain are carried to the cook; and he knows what is expected of him. He chops all these ingredients up into small bits with his butcher knife and prepares to stew them slowly in an iron kettle. There are as many different ways to make this dish as there are cooks. Some may throw in some potatoes, a can of tomatoes, or anything else that is handy. If the eater can tell what's in it, it is not a first-class stew. As the cowboy says, "You throw ever'thing in the pot but the hair, horns, and holler." The longer it is cooked the better it is.

Soft grub: Hotel food, fancy victuals.

Sop: Cowboy's name for gravy.

Sourdough bullet: A slang name for a biscuit, not called this within hearing of the cook.

Sourdough keg: A small wooden keg, usually holding about five gallons, in which the cook kept his sourdough. When getting ready for the coming roundup, the cook put three or four quarts of flour into this keg and added a dash of salt and just enough water to make a medium-thick batter. The keg was then placed in the sun to let the heat ferment the contents for several days. Sometimes a little vinegar or molasses was added to hasten the fermentation.

The first batch of batter was merely to season the keg. After the fermentation was well started, it was poured out, and enough new batter mixed up to fill the keg. Each day it was put into the sun to hasten fermentation and each night it was wrapped in blankets to keep the batter warm and working. Some cooks even slept with their kegs. After several days of this treatment, the dough was ready to use. From then to the end of the season the keg was never cleaned out. Every time the cook took out enough dough for a meal, he put back enough of the flour, salt, and water to replace it. In this way he always had plenty of dough working.

When making up his bread, he simply added enough flour and water to this batter to make a medium-stiff dough. Every wagon cook thought his sourdough the best ever, and he took great pride in his product. An outfit that let anything happen to its sourdough keg was in a bad shape, and most cooks would just about defend their kegs with their lives.

Sourdoughs: Either the plural of sourdough or biscuits.

Sow bosom: Salt pork.

Splatter dabs: Slang name for hot cakes.

Spotted pup: Rice and raisins cooked together.

Squirrel can: A large can used by the cook to throw scraps into. Whenever anything, from a saddle blanket to a spur, is lost, someone jokingly suggests looking for it in the squirrel can.

Staked to a fill: Given a good meal.

Swamp seed: Slang name for rice.

Texas butter: The cowboy's name for gravy. Put some flour into the grease in which the steak was fried and let it bubble and brown, then add hot water and stir until it thickens.

Whistle-berries: The cowboy's name for beans.

Wreck pan: The receptacle for the dirty dishes.

Charles Goodnight, creator of the chuck wagon, was part owner of the JA Ranch in Texas. *Courtesy Library of Congress*

Chapter One
CATTLE TRAILS

The Range Cook's "Holler"

They sing of the puncher—that knight of the range who rounds up the bellerin' steer;
    Who rides at the head of the midnight stampede with nary a symptom of fear.
    They tell of his skill with the six-gun and rope, but nobody mentions the dub
    Who trails the chuck-wagon through desert and plain and never yet failed with the grub!
The weather may find us in rain or in mud; may bake us or sizzle us down;
    The treacherous quicksands may mire us deep, and the leaders and wheelers may drown;
    The blizzards may howl and the hurricane blow, or injuns may camp on our trail,
    But nary excuse will the foreman accept for havin' the chuck-wagon fail.
For off on the range is the puncher who rides through the buck-brush and sage and mesquite,
    With an appetite fierce for the bacon we fry, and the slapjacks we bake him to eat.
    And we must be waitin' with grub smokin' hot when he comes a-clatterin' in,
    No matter what troubles we've bucked up agin, or what our delays may have been.
So in singin' yer songs of the men of the plains who trail it through desert and pine,
    Who rough it from Idaho's borders clear down to the edge of the Mexican line,
    Don't give all the due to the puncher of steers, but chip in some dope of the dub
    Who trails the chuck-wagon in sun or in storm, and never yet failed with the grub!

—E. A. Brininstool, *Trail Dust of a Maverick*, 1914

There were numerous cattle trails all over the West, with a large portion of them originating in Texas. Some of the most frequently used trails were:

- the Chisholm Trail, which ran from Texas, through Oklahoma, and then into Kansas

- the Chisum Trail, which started near Paris, Texas, followed the Pecos River past Roswell, and went to Fort Sumner, New Mexico.

- the Great Western Cattle Trail, which went from Bandera, Texas, through Oklahoma (Indian Territory), into Dodge City, Kansas, and all the way up to the Montana Territory.

There were also smaller trails that ran off the Great Western that went into the Dakota Territory and Wyoming, and the Shawnee Trail, which left from Texas and passed through Indian Territory, Kansas, and Nebraska. It also splintered off into Missouri.

With so many cattle drives occurring in the 1860s, it became harder and harder to feed the ten to twenty men who tended the cattle. That's when Charles Goodnight invented the chuck wagon.

Charles Goodnight who was a Texas Ranger turned cattle rancher in Texas in the 1860s. In 1866 he and fellow rancher, Oliver Loving, created the Goodnight-Loving Trail to move cattle. It originally ran from Texas, through New Mexico, and into Colorado. Loving was killed in 1867, but Goodnight went on to expand the trail into Wyoming. In 1876 he entered into a partnership with Cornelia and John Adair to begin the JA Ranch in Palo Duro Canyon, Texas.

During Goodnight's cattle drives he saw the need for a way to feed the cowboys, so he modified an army surplus Studebaker wagon. He strapped a box on the back and fitted it with cooking supplies like pots, utensils, staples, and more.

The invention changed the experience of the cattle drive for the cowboys on the trail. They also had the added benefit of the cook who ran the chuck wagon. He not only provided them meals, but was their doctor, seamstress, and confidant. Cooks were paid twenty to thirty dollars a month and were affectionately called names like Cookie, Belly-cheater, Greasy Belly, Gut Robber, Sallie, Coosie, Beef-trust, Dog face, Dutch, Beans, Punk, Grease-pot and Whistle-berry.

Staples on the chuck wagon were things that traveled well and didn't spoil. The list included flour, sourdough, salt, brown sugar, beans, rice, cornmeal, dried apples and peaches, baking powder, baking soda, coffee, and airtights, which were canned goods. Airtights included tomatoes, corn, and gallon containers of syrup, which was usually molasses or sorghum. While fresh beef was the main meat, wild game and fish were sometimes available along the trail and during roundups. Bacon grease was used to fry everything, but it also served as the main meat when supplies ran low.

Sometimes the cowboys were treated to dessert, and it usually consisted of cobbler, rehydrated fruit, or fruit pudding. Eggs were rare since they broke so easily, but sometimes the cook and cowboys traded local homesteaders for some.

Most chuck wagon cooks didn't use recipes because they just knew how to cook. Some had

The Chuck Wagon

The *Topeka Capital-Commonwealth* described a chuck wagon in its April 19, 1889, edition: "The most important article in the cowboy's outfit is the chuck wagon . . . It is a common prairie schooner, with hoops over it to stretch a canvas roof on, so that such perishable goods as salt, sugar, and flour can be protected from weather. At the back is a cupboard, where such things as baking powder, pepper, coffee, dishes, etc. are kept. There are pots and frying pans a plenty, and the larder is always well supplied. Bacon is generally preferred to salt pork, and fresh beef is kept constantly on hand by killing a steer from the herd as occasion requires. The owners of the herd supply the food and such tools as shovels, axes, etc." A chuck wagon also included convenient drawers for plates, cups, and utensils. Others stored coffee, bacon, beans, and other chuck. Chuck boxes also had a drawer for a few simple remedies such as liniment, pills, salts, quinine, and calomel. Sometimes the cook might stash a secret bottle of whiskey for his personal use in case of "snake bites."

The chuck wagon was a kitchen-on-the-fly during cattle drives and roundups. Ca. 1900. *Courtesy Library of Congress*

been cooks during the Civil War, and others learned along the way. Since no recipes could be found from the actual chuck wagon days, the 1909 book called *Camping and Camp Cooking* was used to replicate recipes here. Some were modified to use the ingredients the cookie would have had with him or those available during roundups.

On the Trails

Texas cowboy Billy Robinson spent most of his life in Uvalde County. He recalled taking cattle for F. C. Gates into Dodge City, Kansas: "I went up the trail twice to Dodge City, Kansas. It took us seventy-six days to make the trip. We went out from Uvalde up the Main Frio and hit Paint Creek, south Llano, and San Angelo . . . We only traveled six or seven miles a day on the trail on account of the drags. It's a funny thing—when you get to Kansas the drags would be your lead cattle. And milk! We sure had plenty to drink. Everything sure got fat on the trail like as you'd think so. You wouldn't know your own saddle horse by the time you got to Kansas. On that trip we had nine cow-hands and a cook. And we had beans and bacon and bacon and beans. No potatoes. Never had seen a potato or knew what it was. We had rice and dried apples. But we wanted meat, we were used to meat. We had meat about twice or three times except some Antelope meat. Antelope meat isn't near as good as venison. We carried one extra suit of clothes with us but I remember one fellow who never washed his undershirt till he got to Kansas. We carried an overcoat for that was sure

important and that was about all except our leggins and rope. I remember a good woman rider over at Fort Clark who was called Babe Ross. By giminy, she rode horses all the time and she rode after her own stock. No, she wasn't a bit pretty but she sure could ride. They called her the cowboy girl and she was just that. I didn't know much about her but I know she always rode a flea-bitten gray pony and nothing ever got away from her."

In 1898 Tex Bender and C. C. Post published *Ten Years a Cowboy*, a book about cowboys on the trails. They wrote: "Deer and antelope abounded; herds of buffalo were by no means unfrequent, and jack rabbits were everywhere, so that there was lack neither of sport nor meat in variety for the daily fare; and with the addition of corn meal, with which to make bread, coffee and bacon for a change and seasoning."

Texas was full of cowboys because that's where most of the cattle was raised and then herded up north. E. L. Murphy signed on with the Graham Ranch in 1892 and recalled, "My life as a cowhand began when I was 20 years old, down in Travis County, 12 [miles?] west of Austin. There is where I was born, August 25th, 1872, on [?] farm. I learned to ride a hoss at an early age at my native home during the days of my youth. If you wished to [?] to some place those days, you either [?] your axles, [?] hoofed it, or rode a hoss. I hit up the big auger, Mr. Graham, owner of the Graham outfit, for a job when I was 20 years old. That was in 1892. I was a greener then, of course, knew how to make a mess. How did we live? Well, on the drive the chuck wagon carried the chuck . . . On the drive the bellie-cheater was hard put at times to shape the chuck proper, because of the fuel. The drive was always in the fall an' we had, more or less, wet spells of weather.

"The cookie depended on cow chips an' mesquite for fuel an' that don't fire good when wet. He used to keep the coonie loaded when fuel was handy, but it did not hold a great deal an' at times he ran short. So that you tenderfoots may know what a coonie is I shall explain it. It was a cowhide stretched under the wagon an' used to carry wood or any other thing the bellie-cheater wanted to use it for. We snaked for dinner an' had supper after the herd bedded down. Our food run strong to whistle berries, they were the red Mexican variety of beans. They were good food and fine while on the drift or on the range, but while in camp—not so good. In the dog house it became whiffy on the Lee side at times. Next in line was son-of-a-gun stew.

"We always had a good supply of sop, which was made out of bacon grease, flour, water an' a little pepper an' salt. There was always a good supply of lick, either of the black molasses or sorghum brand. [But?] of the sorghum an' bacon grease we made our Charley Taylor (cowboy butter). The only butter we ever saw was the Texas brand that was the good old bacon grease. Now, you understand that we always had all the meat we could call for. The yearlings were handy and also antelope. The black coffee was always ready when we wanted a tin full . . . The chuck was plain rough food, but good. The cowhands always had plenty of leaf lard on their ribs. I have often been chided about the cowhand's big hat and other dress. The greeners

ask, 'Why do the cowboy wear such a big hat?' Well, the answer is simple. The Texas sun required it. If a person is going to stay out in it. The Texas cowhand was as sad as a hound's eye if he was without a good conk cover. He often paid a month's wages, an' that was around $30."

SOP

MAKES ABOUT 2 CUPS

    4 tablespoons bacon grease or butter
    4 tablespoons flour
    2 cups water
    Salt and pepper to taste

Melt bacon grease in a skillet over medium heat.

Add the flour and stir to blend. Cook for 1–2 minutes.

Add the water and cook, stirring, until thick.

Add salt and pepper.

CHARLEY TAYLOR

MAKES 1 CUP

    1 stick butter, room temperature
    2 tablespoons molasses or sorghum

Beat butter and molasses together in a bowl.

Spread on toast, pancakes, or anything you like.

RECIPES ADAPTED BY AUTHOR FROM THE PRECEDING STORY.

Son-of-a-B (Gun) Stew

A rare treat chuck wagon cooks fed their cowhands was son-of-a-gun stew, made when a young calf was killed. Its original name ended with a five-letter word that starts with B.

Nearly everything from the calf was put into the stew, but one cowboy remembered his cookie trying to include something extra. "Next in line was son-of-a-gun stew," recalled E. L. Murphy, who began cowboying for the Graham Ranch west of Austin, Texas, in 1892. "It was made of everything, but the hide an' horns of the critter, but our cheater slipped in a horn at times, so we accused him of it."

Emmerson "Eem" Hurst, whose first ranch outfit was a horse camp run by cattleman C. C. Slaughter's boys in Coppell, Texas, in 1884, praised his cookie's mastery of the son-of-a-gun stew: "The portions of each ingredient is judged by instinct. If you go measuring stuff the stew will sure be spoiled."

An 1865 Texas cowhand, Albert Erwin, recalled, "Our chuck was composed of beans, meat, sourdough and corn bread and a few canned vegetables. We made and drank black coffee by the gallons. When we had canned vegetables, we broke the chuck monotony with son-of-a-gun stew. Also, during the spring, when we castrated the male yearlings, the chuck monotony would be broken with messes of mountain oysters."

TEXAS CORN BREAD

This recipe appeared in a Denver paper in 1898 with the note, "The Texans eat this molasses bread with coffee as a kind of dessert. It rises light and is well-tasting."

MAKES 1 LOAF

- 2 cups yellow cornmeal
- 1 teaspoon baking soda
- Pinch of salt
- 1 cup molasses
- ½ teaspoon butter or lard, melted
- 2 eggs, beaten

Mix the cornmeal, soda, and salt in a large bowl.

Add the molasses, butter, and eggs, and stir until blended.

Pour into a greased square or loaf pan and bake at 400°F for about 25 minutes.

Check for doneness with a toothpick.

RECIPE ADAPTED FROM DENVER'S *WEEKLY NEWS*, JUNE 9, 1898.

SON OF A GUN STEW SUBSTITUTE

Since traditional son of a gun stew contains ingredients many people find off-putting, this beef stew might be a more palatable substitute. Feel free to add any portion of the cow you like!

SERVES 4–6

> Salt and pepper to taste
> Flour for dredging
> 1 pound beef, cubed
> Oil for frying
> 1 turnip, peeled and cubed
> 2 onions, peeled and sliced
> ½ carrot, peeled and diced
> 6–8 small potatoes, peeled and parboiled

Add the salt and pepper to the flour, and dredge the meat in this mixture.

Fry the meat in a small amount of oil over medium-high heat in a large stockpot, until browned. Remove the meat.

Add more oil to the pot if needed, and cook the turnip, onions, and carrot until browned.

Return the meat to the pot and cover with boiling water.

Simmer until the meat is tender, about 2 hours.

Add the potatoes and cook for another 30 minutes.

RECIPE ADAPTED FROM SOUTH DAKOTA'S *ABERDEEN DAILY NEWS*, FEBRUARY 14, 1888.

Sourdough

Sourdough, like so many other things, was created because of a need. Yeast cakes weren't always available, so cooks created their own liquid yeast. They used any combination of potatoes, potato water, hops, salt, sugar, water, and flour to create perpetual or wild yeast. All they had to do was save a little from the original "starter" and refresh it with each use. They didn't call it sourdough; it was simply yeast to them.

Chuck wagon cooks and ranch owners relied on sourdough to make their bread. The starter was renewed almost daily because of the demand for bread and rolls. The word *sourdough* wasn't used to describe bread until around the turn of the century. Bread was just bread with different types of yeast. If an old recipe called for a cup of yeast, it was likely sourdough. If it called for a yeast cake, then it was regular yeast bread. The term also referred to people who were from Alaska or the Pacific Northwest. With time, it evolved from a two-word description to a one-word descriptor.

SOURDOUGH STARTER (MOTHER STARTER)

Getting some starter from a friend is better since you know it will work. If you can't get some from a friend, then here's a recipe to get you started. There's also a link at the end of the book for a free Oregon Trail starter.

MAKES 1½ CUPS

2 tablespoons bread flour
1½ tablespoons warm water (If your tap water has a funny odor or taste, use bottled water.)

Place the flour and water in a wide-mouthed canning jar or other glass container.

Cover the container loosely with plastic wrap and let stand at room temperature (65°–75°F) for 24 hours.

For the next 6 days, do the same thing: Add the flour and water in the same amounts as before, cover the mixture, and let it sit again.

After the third day you should see tiny bubbles on the surface, which indicates that yeast is developing and producing gas.

At the end of seventh day you should have about 1½ cups of starter, and you can transfer it to a permanent glass container and refrigerate it. Place plastic wrap on the top and lightly screw on a canning jar lid, but not too tight. You should be able to push on the plastic wrap. Doing this allows the starter to breathe. There is now enough starter to bake a loaf of bread and have some left over to keep feeding for next time.

Store in the refrigerator. If not used at least every 2 weeks, it may separate and turn slightly gray. The gray liquid is called hooch and should be poured off before using the starter.

FRESH STARTER

Recipes should begin with a fresh starter, so follow this recipe the day before you bake.

    1 cup mother starter
    ¾ cup warm water (If your tap water has a
        funny odor or taste, use bottled water.)
    1 cup flour

Place the mother starter, warm water, and flour in a nonmetallic bowl. Stir until blended; don't worry about lumps.

Cover the bowl loosely and allow it to sit overnight at room temperature.

The next day, stir the mixture down and measure out the amount of fresh starter needed for your recipe.

Return the remainder to your refrigerated storage container, stirring it in well; doing so "feeds" your mother starter. You must feed it at least once a month or it will die.

SOURDOUGH BREAD

MAKES 1 LOAF

    1 cup fresh starter
    ½ cup warm water (If your tap water has a
        funny odor or taste, use bottled water.)
    1 tablespoon sugar
    ½ teaspoon salt

    2 tablespoons dry milk powder
    1 tablespoon vegetable oil or melted
        shortening
    Flour to make a stiff dough (2–3 cups)
    1 tablespoon butter, melted

Place the starter, water, sugar, salt, milk powder, and oil in a large nonmetallic bowl, and stir.

Incorporate 1 cup of the flour and let the dough relax for 15 minutes.

Gradually add the remaining flour until you have a stiff—but not sticky—dough.

Turn out the dough and knead well, adding flour as necessary until the dough is smooth and stands about a third (or more) as high as it is wide when resting.

Place the dough in a greased bowl, cover, and let rise in a warm, draft-free place until doubled in size—about 1–2 hours.

Punch the dough down and let rest 15 minutes. Shape into a loaf and place into a greased, 9 x 5 x 3-inch bread pan. Brush the top with melted butter. Let rise until the top of the dough is almost even with top edge of the pan—about 1 hour.

Bake for 45 minutes at 375°F. Turn out immediately onto a rack.

RECIPES ADAPTED FROM THE SAN FRANCISCO *DAILY EVENING BULLETIN*, NOVEMBER 17, 1877.

Mrs. Burks

Amanda Burks was a sophisticated lady who followed her husband on cattle drives from Texas. She was known as the "Queen of the Old Trail." She and her husband used the Chisholm Trail, but Mrs. Burks referred to it as the "Old Kansas Trail." When she took it in 1871, the trail ended in Newton, Kansas. She was later interviewed about her experience and recalled, "Fuel was very scarce because of these [prairie] fires and the cook often had to go miles to get enough to cook a meal. We crossed many nice cool streams whose banks were covered with wild plums. I noticed the ripe ones first when crossing the Washita, and wanted to stop to gather some. Mr. Burks wasn't ready to stop, so he told me that the Indians were very troublesome at this place, and I needed no coaxing to start the horses on. Later, when we came to the Canadian River, the red, blue, and yellow plums were so tempting I had one of the Mexicans stop with me to gather some. We wandered farther away from the buggy than I realized, and when we had gone back a short way I thought the horses had run away and left us. I was panic-stricken, but the Mexican insisted that we go farther upstream, and we soon found the horses standing just as they were left. I forgot my scare when the cook served me with delicious plum pie made from the fruit I had gathered.

"Being the only woman in camp, the men rivaled each other in attentiveness to me. They were always on the lookout for something to please me, a surprise of some delicacy of the wild fruit, or prairie chicken, or antelope tongue."

Her obituary was lengthy, and it appeared in the *Dallas Morning News* on September 16, 1931. It read:

Amanda Burks
Queen of Old Trail
Amanda Burks, 92, Dies at Her
Ranch In Buggy She Followed Herd to
Abilene, Kan., in '71.
SAN ANTONIO. Texas. Sept 15 (AP).-
Mrs. Amanda Burks. 92. Ranch woman and known as 'the queen of the old trail' died at 5 p. m. Tuesday at La Mott Ranch twenty-five miles east of Cotulla, where she had lived since 1876. This word was received late Tuesday by George W. Saunders, president of the Old Trail Drivers' Association, of which Mrs. Burks was a member, having gone with a herd of cattle to Abilene, Kan., in 1871, riding all the way in a buggy. Mrs. Burks moved to La Mott Ranch, which now consists of 43.000 acres, from Nueces County with her husband, W. F. Burks. His death occurred a year later, and since that time Mrs. Burks has shouldered the entire management of the property.

Moved to Ranch In 1876.
The funeral services will be held at 4 p.m. Wednesday at the ranch home and burial will be in the old cemetery on the ranch. Mr. Saunders and Mrs. Saunders

and many old-time cattlemen from San Antonio will attend the funeral. After Mr. and Mrs. Burks moved to the ranch in 1876, they hauled all ranch supplies from Corpus Christi until the railroad was built into Cotulla in 1882. During this time they were troubled with Indians and rustlers and lost many cattle and horses. Their first residence was built of cypress lumber, which had previously been, used in a storehouse at Banquette Nueces County. This building still is standing on the ranch and is in use by tenants.

Has Enlarged Her Holdings.

Since her husband's death, Mrs. Burks has bought more land and added to the original ranch, which at that time consisted of only four sections. The property is all well fenced, and cross fenced and is stocked with cattle, goats and horses. In 1890 Mrs. Burks bought the first courthouse of La Salle County, which stood near old Fort Ewell. The building was on the old Stuart ranch, which was called Guajaco, and was used for many years as a stage stand. It is now used as a tenant house. In 1889 Mrs. Burks bought 60.000 feet of lumber from the Perkins mill, in Lake Charles, La., had it shipped to Cotulla and hauled from there to her ranch. The operation consumed seven months. The large modem home now ranch headquarters was built in 1900. It faces a large lake bordered with live oaks.

Rode Trail from Banquette.

In 1925 Mrs. Burks rode in the trail drivers' parade here and was in the receiving line at the Gunter Hotel when the pony express riders arrived. She was but a young woman when she accompanied her husband on his trail drive to the Kansas markets with 4,000 beeves. The start was made from Banquette. The Burks had moved to the latter place from Angelina County, where they settled following the close of the Civil War. The journey to Kansas consumed three months. She was accompanied by a negro servant, who rode horse back. When she tired of the buggy she would exchange places with him.

Has Been Boss of Ranch.

On this trip she swam her horse across swollen streams, experienced a prairie fire and witnessed numerous storms and accompanying stampedes of cattle. When her husband died her nearest neighbor lived eight miles away. However, undeterred, she took over the management of the large property, and for fifty-three years has been recognized 'boss,' although of late years she has been assisted by her nephew, Jack Baylor, grandson of Gen. John R. Baylor, who was born on the ranch and has lived there since. Mrs. Jim Bell a niece of Mrs. Burks, also lives on the ranch, as does the latter's daughter, Virginia.

BAKED PRAIRIE CHICKEN

SERVES 4–6

    1 whole chicken, 3–4 pounds
    Salt and pepper to taste
    2 teaspoons marjoram
    2 cups dressing (See recipe in chapter 5.)
    6–8 slices bacon

Season the bird inside and out with salt, pepper, and marjoram. Stuff with dressing.

Drape the bacon over the breast-side of the chicken.

Bake in a tightly covered pan at 350°F for about 1¾–2 hours.

Uncover for the last 20 minutes to brown the top. Check for doneness with a meat thermometer inserted between the leg joints. Internal temperature should be between 175° and 180°F. Allow to rest 5–10 minutes before carving.

RECIPE ADAPTED FROM THE *KANSAS HOME COOK BOOK,* 1874.

The Chuck Wagon Cookie

Being a chuck wagon cook in the Old West was a tough job. He only had certain ingredients to cook with and sometimes had to deal with unruly cowhands.

You know the old saying, "Never bring a knife to a gunfight"? Well, that's just what Frenchy the cookie should have remembered. John Baker, who was born a Texan in 1850, but traveled to Wyoming, the Dakotas, and New Mexico on cattle drives, remembered Frenchy: "The belly-cheater on the Holt outfit was a fellow called Frenchy and a top cookie. Frenchy and a fellow named Hinton got into it over Hinton digging into the chuck box which was against Frenchy's rule as it was with any good cookie. They did not want the waddies messing up the chuck box. Hinton seemed to get a kick out of seeing Frenchy get riled and would mess around the chuck box.

"The evening that the fight took place Hinton walked past Frenchy and dove into the chuck box. Frenchy went after Hinton with a carving knife and Hinton drew his gun. Frenchy was hit several times and Hinton was cut in a number of places . . . Cookie kept diving in close and slashing, finally he drove the knife into Hinton's breast and they both went to the ground and died a few minutes later."

On the lighter side: So, this guy lost his pants to a couple of cows . . . I bet you are waiting for the punch line. Well, there isn't one—this is a true story! The multitasking Julius McKinney was preparing the noonday meal while also washing his clothes. Not wanting to be naked, he fashioned a shirt and pants from used cornsacks. After finishing up a pan of biscuit dough, he went to check his clothes. To his dismay, they were gone. Looking downriver he saw two cows chewing on his clothes. Texas waddy Bill Kellis reported, "These two bovines were noted as the worst chewers on the ranch." McKinney tried to chase the cows, but to no avail. Kellis noted, "He could never face the boys all dressed up in his corn sacks; they would razz him to death. Knowing that he could never be seen in the corn sack suit he determined to get away somehow, so he mounted one of the wagon mules and rode for San Angelo, fifty miles away, the nearest place at which he could purchase a shirt and pants."

Some of the belly-cheaters were a little rough around the edges, as Texas waddy E. L. remembered: "The belly-cheater would have chow ready before daylight in the morning. He would yell, 'come an' get yo'r hell,' about the break of day. Sometimes he would yell, 'washup snakes an' come to it.' When he yelled that we always calculated that he had a fair to middlin' dish of nourishment shaped up . . . The bread was sourdough gun wadding an' often we were treated to saddle blankets. You greeners call it griddle cakes."

The chuck wagon cook was affectionately called many names, including Cookie. He also served as mother, doctor, seamstress, and more. *Courtesy Library of Congress*

Gun wadding is cowboy slang for a loaf of light bread, according to Scott Gregory's book, *Sowbelly and Sourdough*. *Saddle blanket* is the cowboy name for a large pancake.

Cowboys had their own lingo for many things, including pancakes or flannel cakes. They referred to them as saddle blankets.

FLANNEL CAKES, NO. 2

MAKES ABOUT 12 MEDIUM PANCAKES

> 2 cups milk, warm
> 1 packet yeast
> ½ teaspoon salt
> 2½ cups flour
> 1½ tablespoons butter
> ¼ cup milk
> 1 egg

Pour the warm milk into a large glass or earthenware bowl. Whisk in the yeast and salt. Add the flour and stir to combine.

Cover with plastic and allow to sit in a warm place (like a microwave) overnight.

In the morning, warm (do not boil) the butter and the milk in a small saucepan. Add to the flour and yeast mixture and stir. Beat in the egg.

Heat a griddle or nonstick frying pan over medium-high heat. Grease with shortening or butter. Pour the batter into pancakes and cook until bubbles form.

Flip with a spatula and cook a minute longer. Serve with additional butter and syrup.

RECIPE ADAPTED FROM *MANUAL FOR ARMY COOKS*, 1879. THE RECIPE WAS DEVELOPED BY THE COOKS AT FORT OMAHA, NEBRASKA.

Texas Cattlemen

Aaron Lloyd Turner was born in Leon County, Texas, to South Carolina and Georgia parents in 1850. His parents' land was at the juncture of the Navasota River and the Camino Real. His great-grandson, western author Steve Turner, shared, "My great grandfather took cattle to Sedalia in '66; then Abilene beginning in '68; one herd to Caldwell, and later, up the Western trail to Dodge. He was innovative and hauled buffalo hides from Ft. Griffin, TX to Dodge, and brought back goods to sell to stores and ranches. He eventually began to bring back barbed wire and implements necessary to dig/erect windmills."

Aaron Turner drove from 1,000 to 1,600 head of cattle each year with some of his own and some of his neighbors'. The cowhands usually bought in some of their own stock to add to the herd. He also caught maverick cattle out of the cane breaks and river bottoms of Leon, Limestone, and Robertson Counties. Turner took the herd northwest following the Brazos to pick up cattle belonging to Captain Benjamin C. Tyus. They then crossed the Red River at Red River Crossing at Preston, Texas, and on up the Shawnee Trail through the Nations. They crossed the corner of Kansas into Missouri to the railhead at Sedalia, in June 1866.

From 1868 to 1874 Turner and his outfit drove cattle up Chisholm Trail to Abilene, Kansas, to the Kansas Pacific Railroad. He had twelve men on the drive, including the cook's helper/wrangler. Their chuck wagon was built into a Studebaker freight wagon. According to Steve Turner, "I don't know who the cook was, but they ate beans and corn bread with coffee twice a day. They kept jerky and corn pones in their pocket and washed it down with canteen water for the midday meal. Sometimes they would have beef, if they had to kill a crippled one and the cook had time to fix it and would make chili or stew. If they traded a homesteader they might have fresh vegetables, eggs rarely, and they couldn't afford flour for biscuits until the return trip from Sedalia. After that, they often had biscuits in the morning and corn bread at night. Once in a while they might have venison, turkey or even fish. Dessert? Maybe weekly, cobbler of local berries or fruit, or dried apples, apricots, peaches (dried apricot cobbler was a favorite of Aaron's), Arbuckles' Coffee (already ground and roasted, lightly coated with film of dry egg whites and sugar to form into a block)." Meals were eaten on speckled enamelware plates and bowls. After use, each person, including the boss, was expected to scrape unused food off the enamelware into a slop bucket and throw his dishes into a "wreck pan."

CHILI

SERVES 4

2–3 dried Ancho chile peppers or 2–3 tablespoons chili powder
⅓ pound bacon, diced
1 pound beef or venison, cubed
1 medium onion, diced
1 teaspoon salt
3 garlic cloves, diced
1 large can tomatoes, chopped

If using dried peppers, soak them in water until soft. To reduce the heat, cut off the tops and remove the seeds. Wear gloves to handle the peppers, and do not touch your eyes after handling chiles until you've washed your hands.

Dice the peppers and set aside.

Melt the bacon fat in a large dutch oven over medium-high heat.

Add the beef or venison, onions, and salt, and cook for 5–7 minutes or until the meat is browned.

Add the garlic, and cook for a minute more.

Add tomatoes and peppers. Cook for an hour over low heat and then test for seasoning.

Continue cooking uncovered until meat is tender or about another hour.

RECIPE ADAPTED FROM WALKER PROPERTIES ASSOCIATION RECIPE BOOKLET (AUSTIN, TX), 1918.

FRUIT COBBLER

Cobblers were called many things during the nineteenth century, including duff, slump, pudding, charlotte, and pie.

SERVES 4–6

- 4 cups fresh or canned apples, apricots, peaches, or berries
- 2 cups flour
- ½ cup sugar
- 2 teaspoons baking powder
- 1 cup milk

Wash, peel, and/or pit the fruit and place into a greased dutch oven.

Combine dry ingredients in a bowl, and mix.

Add the milk and stir just until moistened.

Spread over the fruit and bake covered in a 375°F oven for 40–45 minutes or until done.

RECIPE ADAPTED FROM THE OMAHA, NEBRASKA, *WORLD-HERALD*, OCTOBER 11, 1896.

Cobblers like these were the most common desserts on the trail, if there were any desserts at all.

BAKED PEACHES

SERVES 4–6

6 peaches
½ cup sugar
12 teaspoons butter

Peel the peaches, cut them in half, and remove the pits.

Place into a buttered, ovenproof dish so they all touch.

Completely cover with sugar and place a teaspoon of butter on each peach half.

Bake at 325°F for about 30 minutes or until tender. Serve warm or cold.

RECIPE ADAPTED FROM THE AUGUST 14, 1898, *DALLAS MORNING NEWS*.

Chapter Two
ROUNDUPS

Finale of the Puncher

When the last great herd has vanished,
    And the open range is gone;
    When the cattle are all banished,
    And their numbers are withdrawn,
    When the brandin' days are over,
    And the ropin' is all through,
    Then it is we'll sit and wonder
    What's the cowpunch goin' to do?
When the cowman comes to sever
    What connections he had left'
    When the trail-herds pass forever,
    And there ain't a cayuse left;
    When the ol' chuckwagon rumbles
    O'er the ridges out of view,
    And the cook quits yellin' "Grub pile!"
    What's the puncher goin' to do?
When the squealin', bruckin' bronco
    Has become an ol' plow nag;
    When the saddle and the poncho
    Hand up in an ol' grain bag;

When his bits and spurs are rustin'.
    And his gun is useless, too,
    And there's no more round-ups startin'
    What's the puncher goin' to do?
When the last night-herdin's finished,
    And he's seen his last stampede,
    When the bunkhouse gang's diminished,
    And of brand-irons there's no need;
    When the ol' worn yellow slicker
    Is put by for store-duds new,
    And his chaps have been discarded,
    What's the puncher goin' to do?
When there ain't no wild west longer;
    When the plains are seas of grain,
    And the nesters crowd in stronger,
    Till the cowman can't remain;
    When ol' life's but a vision
    To which he must bid adieu,
    Tell me, oh, my ol' range pardners,
    What's the puncher goin' to do?

—E. A. Brininstool, *Trail Dust of a Maverick*, 1914

Before the days of barbed wire and fencing, cattle were allowed to roam free and graze until spring-time, when the ranchers needed their cattle all together to get them to market. Roundups were conducted two times per year for different reasons. The spring roundup allowed the rancher to collect the cattle that had wandered over the open lands.

During the spring roundup cattle were also branded with a temporary trail brand. Trail-branding was the ranchers' way of claiming ownership during cattle drives, before their animals were sold in the cow towns. Not every single cow on the ranch was sent to market; many were "cut" and held back from the herd going to market.

The fall roundup allowed ranchers to gather their cattle from sometimes miles away. Many times cowboys from multiple nearby ranches traveled together. Since all the cattle grazed openly, oftentimes cattle from different ranches were mixed together.

Each rancher would send a chuck wagon and cowboys to round the cattle up and return them to their ranch. Before the invention of the chuck wagon, each cowboy took a tin cup for coffee and a bread pan or tin plate to eat on. The cooks varied in their cooking techniques and what they cooked. What and how they cooked were often dictated by their locations. Some cooks used a wet, sourdough starter to make bread and biscuits; others used a form of baking soda (*saleratus*) to make theirs. Some cooked their meat by cutting it into pieces and frying it. But sometimes cowboys preferred to roast their own on sticks over open wood coals.

According to Texas cowboy Neal Watts, "All the ranchers in the region took part in the roundup. Then all the strays were separated, the calves branded and the cattle counted. As the roundup proceeded from one section to another, more or less strays belonging to different sections would be encountered. Each rancher had some waddies, called 'reps', in the roundup crew who looked after their ranch's cattle. The cattle would stray off of their home range during storms, or when the grazing became scarce. Otherwise, the cattle would stay within the vicinity of their own range. The herd would graze far away, at times perhaps several miles, but towards late evening they would start drifting towards their bedding ground. They bedded near the waterhole and salt licks."

Roundup Grub

One early cowboy named Ike Fridge had ridden with Colonel Chisum beginning in 1869. In those days, the chuck wagon was unheard of and cowboys made their own meals. They "broiled" their meat over hot wood coals, and green sticks sufficed as the grill. Their bread was made from flour, cold water, salt, and baking soda. To bake it they wrapped it around a freshly cut branch and held it over the fire until done.

Cowhand John Hardgreaves Crawford of Elk, Texas, recalled his days as a cowboy. He had his first experiences in "cow hunting" in 1867 and 1868, and his equipment was a pony and saddle. He recalled days in West Texas in 1878, "Cattle often

In the nineteenth century, the cooking term "broiling" meant cooking meat over a flame.

drifted a hundred miles. During the spring round-up cattle were gathered as before. It required a month or six weeks for each round-up. The ranch outfits would start about the first of May; they used a wagon equipped with a grub box, the lid of this box was used for a table. Provisions were kept in the box. They ate beans, bacon, coffee, and killed and cooked a calf every two or three days. Made coffee in buckets. Had a boss over the cook wagon. They built a fire in a trench and threw branding irons across this on which vessels were placed to cook. They cooked a big pot of beans, or stew and put a big spoon or fork in it. Each ranch-hand helped himself to the coffee, bread and stew, then they would go off fifteen or twenty feet from the fire to eat. They would get their bed and make it down by their saddles. Saddles were used as pillows. Horses were hobbled out for the night."

Cowboy Coffee

While coffee was a staple in every camp, coffee beans weren't always available. Ingenious cookies learned to brew coffee with substitute beans, using cornmeal, barley, or wheat. Jonathan Sanford Ater lived in Texas in the late 1800s. He recalled, "Coffee was made from parched corn, okra, diced sweet potatoes, wheat, or rye."

Coffee and eggs sound good, right? How about eggs in your coffee? It's true—brewing a pot of coffee was much different back in the day. The grounds were cooked in a pot with no filter or strainer. Adding eggshells to the pot was a way to keep the coffee grounds at the bottom.

A native Texan, W. H. Thomas worked as a cowhand in the 1870s and later remembered the camp coffee: "One thing you could depend on at any time of the day or night, especially in the winter and that was the blackest coffee that can be made. I can just see the old coffee pot now, big enough to hold a couple gallons at a time, and a couple of egg shells floating around in it to settle the grounds. We never got but few eggs to eat and we always accused cookie of carrying the same egg shells around from year to year."

A cowboy named Charles Siringo turned his cowboy experiences into a book. He told his first tales in 1885, but then wrote an expanded version in 1919 called *A Lone Star Cowboy*. He wrote, "We always started the day's work at the first peep of day and never thought of eating a noon meal. Often it would be pitch dark when we arrived in camp, where a warm camp fire meal awaited us. These meals were made up of meat from a fat heifer calf, with corn bread, molasses, and black coffee. The Negro cook, who drove the mess-wagon, generally had two kinds of meat, the calf ribs broiled before the camp fire, and a large dutch oven full of loin, sweet-breads, and heart mixed with flour gravy. For breakfast we often had pork and beans which had been simmering over hot coals all night. In those days, knives and forks were seldom used in the cow camps; each cowboy used his bowie knife or pocket knife to eat with."

Arbuckles' was synonymous with coffee to the cowboys. Up until the Civil War coffee was purchased green, roasted over the fire until just the right color, and then ground. Then it was boiled to make coffee. Two brothers changed all that in the 1860s.

John and Charles Arbuckle initiated a new concept in the coffee industry when they started selling roasted coffee in one-pound packages. The Arbuckle Brothers were able to roast a coffee that was a consistently fine-quality product. It was also the first to be packaged in one-pound bags. Arbuckles' Ariosa blend became so popular in the Old West that most cowboys didn't even know there was any other. The Arbuckle Brothers enjoyed immense success into the twentieth century and often made the papers. By the late 1930s, the company was broken up by the family, and the only company brand that survived was Yuban. In 1974 Pat and Denny Willis revived the Arbuckle name and have been roasting Ariosa coffee just like the Arbuckle Brothers did a century ago.

COWBOY COFFEE

SERVES 8

    8 cups water
    8 tablespoons ground coffee

Boil the water in a large saucepan.

Add the coffee and cover.

Lower the heat to simmer for 15 minutes.
Simmer longer for stronger coffee, but no more
than 30 minutes. The grounds will settle as it is
simmering.

RECIPE ADAPTED FROM *CAMPING AND CAMP COOKING*, 1909.

There were no cook stoves
on the trail, so everything,
including coffee, was cooked
over an open flame.

PORK AND NAVY BEANS

SERVES 8–10

  2 cups navy beans
  1 teaspoon salt
  Pepper to taste
  ½ pound salt pork, quartered
  2 tablespoons molasses

Soak beans overnight in water. The next day, rinse and drain.

Place into a large dutch oven or stockpot and cover with water.

Bring to a boil over high heat.

Drain and place in a baking dish. Salt and pepper the beans, and stir.

Place the pork in the center of the beans and then top with the molasses.

Cover and bake at 325°F for 5 hours or until tender.

Note: You can also make these in a slow cooker. After soaking the beans all night, place all the ingredients in the slow cooker and cook overnight or for at least 8 hours on low.

RECIPE ADAPTED FROM MISSOURI'S *KANSAS CITY TIMES*, DECEMBER 19, 1886.

BROILED (GRILLED) BEEF RIBS

SERVES 6–8

  2 pounds beef short ribs
  Salt and pepper to taste

Heat your coals or grill to medium-high heat.

Season ribs with salt and pepper, then sear the ribs on one side for about 10 minutes and then on the other side for another 10 minutes.

Allow to rest for about 5 minutes, and then slice thinly.

RECIPE CREATED BY AUTHOR BASED ON THE STORY PAGE 34.

The *Anaconda Standard* ran a story called, "The Montana Roundup As It Is." It included many details on Montana cowboys, including the food they ate during round-ups. It stated, "The food is good, of variety, well cooked and of unlimited quantity. Bread, biscuits, coffee, tea, sugar, condensed milk, fresh meat, vegetables, canned goods, hominy, beans, rice, puddings and pies are the everyday fare, and no one lacks for appetite."

A Cookie Named Dutch

Avery Barrow was a cowboy who worked on the Tonk Baker ranch in McLennan County, Texas, in the 1870s. "One other pleasant thing about the jew-sharp outfit was the camp cook. We had a good one, 'Dutch' Meyers took pride in his work. To get him doing extra touches all we had to do was swell him on his meals. He would raise like a boil and take extra pains fixing the chuck. Murray use to say, 'the belly-cheater' became very arduous if you give him a chinning. Dutch made some of the best sour-dough bread I have ever ate. Bread, beans, stewed dried fruit, was what we lived on. The cookie would fix the beans different ways. He could fix a Boston baked dish of beans that was fitting to eat, also, fried pies out of the stewed fruit. When it comes to broiling steaks, 'Dutch' had the knack down pat. He would get his camp fire hot slap the steaks into it for a minute, which seared them on the outside. Then he would pull the meat away and let it cook slowly. Of course the beef was off of a fat yearling a good meat to start off with."

STEWED APPLES

This recipe uses fresh apples to save time, even though the original recipe called for dried apples.

SERVES 4–6

    4 cups peeled, cored, and sliced apples
    ½ cup white sugar
    ½ cup brown sugar
    2 cups water

Place all the ingredients in a pot large enough to hold them. Stir and bring to a boil. Reduce the heat to medium, cover, and cook until the apples are tender, about 30–45 minutes. Add additional hot water if needed to continue cooking the apples.

RECIPE ADAPTED FROM THE CLARKSVILLE, TEXAS, *STANDARD*, JANUARY 30, 1880.

There was nothing fancy when it came to food being cooked on the open range. Fresh beef was salt-and-peppered and seared lightly on each side.

GRILLED STEAK

SERVES 4

4 (1-inch thick) T-bone or Porterhouse steaks
Salt and pepper to taste

Get your coals or grill hot. If using coals, make sure they are white.

Allow the steaks to rest on the counter for about 20 minutes to almost room temperature.

Season the steaks with salt and pepper.

Place the steaks on the grill and sear them, uncovered, for 3–4 minutes on one side for medium rare. Do not press or move the steaks.

After the desired cooking time is reached, flip the steaks and grill for 2 minutes uncovered.

After 2 minutes, turn the heat to low and cover for another 2 minutes. Allow steak to rest 5 minutes before serving.

RECIPE CREATED BY THE AUTHOR BASED ON THE DESCRIPTION PAGE 37.

"Come-a-Runnin' You Snakes!"

Edward F. Jones was born in Indian Territory and landed a job with the BO Ranch in Texas. He recalled his time with them, "When I hit the BO outfit, I thought I was a regular. Of course, I could throw a loop some, and ride fairly well but I was nothing more than a scissor bill. John Petrie was the top screw at the time, and it was him I hit up for a nesting place. It was late of day and he said, 'Well, kid, cool your saddle and put your nose in the chuck trough. After you have attended to those duties, we'll gab a spell about the matter.' It was not long 'til the belly-cheater yelled, 'Come a-running you snakes, and get it.'

"That call had a pleasant sound because I had nothing but a Spanish meal since morning and was gaunt. The cookie gave us broiled steak, baked beans, soda sinkers, stewed prunes, and all the Texas butter, sop, and black coffee we desired. After I had packed the chuck 'til my tape worm quit yelling, the top screw says to me, 'Let's adjourn to the dog house where we can chaw the rag a spell.' We moseyed over to the bunkhouse and sat down while he began to get my history."

STEWED PRUNES

SERVES 4–6

    1 pound dried prunes, pitted
    2 quarts water
    4 tablespoons sugar

Place prunes, water, and sugar in a large dutch oven.

Bring to a boil and cook until half the water is gone.

Reduce heat to simmer and cook for about an hour.

RECIPE ADAPTED FROM *SCAMMELL'S CYCLOPEDIA OF VALUABLE RECEIPTS*, 1897.

SODA BISCUITS (SINKERS)

SERVES 6–8

2½ cups flour
½ teaspoon baking soda
½ teaspoon salt
1 tablespoon lard or butter
1 cup buttermilk

Combine the flour, soda, and salt together in a large bowl.

Cut in the lard or butter to form pea-sized pieces.

Add the buttermilk and stir just to combine. Do not overbeat.

Gently knead one or two times on a heavily floured surface.

Roll out to ½-inch thickness. Place in a greased skillet or baking pan.

Bake at 450°F for 10–15 minutes or until golden.

RECIPE ADAPTED FROM TEXAS'S *DENISON DAILY NEWS*, MARCH 3, 1878.

Bread items like biscuits were often put in the cowboys' saddlebags so they had something to eat during lunchtime when they were away from camp.

Never Better

W. H. Thomas, the coffee connoisseur we met earlier, made his way to Graham, Texas, in the 1880s and met Lyt Johnson, who owned a cattle ranch. He recalled, "While I was working for old Lyt, I got the thrill of eating at the chuck wagon during the roundup. Eating around a chuck wagon is the best eating in the world. Nothing special, but good solid food like whistle berries, beef, sow belly strips, and some of the best sop in the world can be made from the grease you get from fried sow belly. . . . We had a good cookie on Lyt's place, though. If everything was favorable, you could depend on a slice of pie two or three times a week, sometimes more.

BUTTERMILK PIE

MAKES 1 PIE

> 1 cup buttermilk
> 2 eggs
> ¾ cup sugar
> 1 teaspoon cornstarch
> Juice and grated rind of half a lemon
> 1 (8-inch) piecrust, unbaked

Combine buttermilk, eggs, sugar, cornstarch, lemon juice, and rind in a large bowl. Mix until blended.

Pour into piecrust (See recipe later in this chapter.) and bake at 350°F for about 35–40 minutes. A knife should come out clean when done.

RECIPE ADAPTED FROM THE *FREDERICKSBURG* (TEXAS) *HOME KITCHEN COOK BOOK*, 1916.

TEXAS PECAN PIE

MAKES 1 PIE

    1 cup sugar
    1 cup milk
    3 eggs, beaten
    1 tablespoon flour
    ½ cup pecans, chopped fine
    1 piecrust (See recipe on facing page.)

Combine the first 5 ingredients in a large bowl.

Pour into the piecrust and bake at 350°F for 40–45 minutes or until the center is set. A knife should come out clean when done.

RECIPE ADAPTED FROM THE *DALLAS MORNING NEWS*, JANUARY 23, 1898.

This Texas pecan pie includes milk, which is a little different than traditional southern recipes.

PIECRUST

MAKES 2 CRUSTS

4 cups flour
½ teaspoon salt
1 tablespoon baking powder
1 cup butter or lard
¾ cup water

Combine flour, salt, and baking powder in a large bowl.

Cut the butter in with a pastry cutter or two knives until the butter is pebble size.

Add the water and mix until blended. Add more water a few drops at a time if needed.

Mix just enough to form a ball. Wrap in plastic wrap and chill for about an hour, if possible. Roll crust on a floured surface, turning the pastry so it doesn't stick.

RECIPE ADAPTED FROM THE *FREDERICKSBURG* (TEXAS) *HOME KITCHEN COOK BOOK*, 1916.

A New Cowboy

Texas cowboy John Childers got his first job at the AH Ranch. He recalled, "My first job on a cow outfit was with the 'ZH,' owned by an Eastern corporation called the [Guscatine?] Cattle Company. The ZH was one of the large outfits ranging in the No-Man's-Land and its brand was carried by 60,000 or more cattle. Everything about the camp was kept in excellent shape. There was no slip-shod methods about the work or operation of the ranch. The headquarters had a well-kept ranch house, chuck wagons with the best of cooks. The remuda was stocked with the best of cow-work trained horses that could be obtained. When I started work I was in range language a greener. My starting wages were $25 per month for the first year. Thereafter they were $35 to $40 per month . . . The general roundups were held each year in the spring and fall. The affairs were called a general roundup and all cow camps in the range territory would join into one outfit, operating under one roundup boss. During this roundup the country would be thoroughly combed for cattle, one section at a time. . . . It required three months to accomplish the work and during this time we lived on a chuck wagon life. Slept in the open, rolled in our blankets. Our food was cooked over a camp fire and consisted of canned vegetables, dried fruit, beef and some pastry. We had some bacon and to vary the meat occasionally some of us would kill some game. Buffalos were still existing in rather large numbers and we ate a lot of choice cuts of buffalo meat."

PEACH PIE

MAKES 1 PIE

8 peaches, peeled, pitted, and sliced
½ cup sugar
¼ cup flour
2 piecrusts
Whipped cream

Combine peaches, sugar, and flour together in a bowl. Mix until coated.

Line a pie pan with 1 piecrust and pour the peaches into it.

Cover with the second crust.

Pinch the crusts together. Bake in a 350°F oven for about 30–40 minutes, until golden.

Serve with whipped cream.

RECIPE ADAPTED FROM THE *IDAHO DAILY STATESMAN*, SEPTEMBER 8, 1889.

Experience Becomes a Book

Although George Henty wasn't a cowboy, his relative in New Mexico was. He used the relative's life story to write the book *Redskin and Cow-boy* back in 1894. He claimed everything in the book, with the exception of a few incidents, was factual. He wrote, "The bread was baked in iron pans. The dough was made of flour and water with a mixture of saleratus, which took the place of yeast, and caused the dough to rise. The pans were placed in the wood embers, a quantity of which were piled upon the flat iron lid, so that the bread was baked equally on all sides. Meat was cut into steaks and fried, those of the men who preferred it cutting off chunks of the meat and grilling or roasting them on sticks over the fire.

"Once or twice a week there was duff or plum-pudding. The cook was up long before daybreak preparing breakfast, and the men started as soon as it was light. Directly after the meal was over, plates, pots, and pans were washed and packed in the waggon, the horses or mules harnessed, and he started for the spot named as the evening camping ground, where he had his fires lighted and the meal well on its way by the time the cow-boys arrived. A good deal more meat than was required was cooked at breakfast, and each man before he started on his day's work, cut off a chunk of bread and meat for his mid-day meal."

FRIED STEAK

SERVES 4–6

    Flour
    Salt and pepper to taste
    1 pound eye round steak, sliced thin
    Butter or lard

Combine the flour, salt, and pepper. Dredge the steaks in the flour.

Heat a frying pan over medium-high heat and add butter or lard.

Fry the steaks, a few at a time, in the butter or lard until golden-brown on each side.

RECIPE ADAPTED FROM THE *FREDERICKSBURG* (TEXAS) *HOME KITCHEN COOK BOOK*, 1916.

BERRY DUFF

SERVES 6–8

    4 cups raspberries, blackberries, or blueberries
    Sugar to taste
    Soda biscuit dough (See recipe earlier in this chapter.)

Place berries in a greased baking dish and sprinkle with sugar.

Spread biscuit dough over the top to cover the berries.

Cover and bake for about 30 minutes at 350°F or until topping is done.

RECIPE ADAPTED FROM THE *KANSAS HOME COOK BOOK*, 1874.

Chapter Three

AT THE RANCH

Most larger ranches had bunkhouses, which served as the cowboys' residence while they lived on the ranch and were not out on roundups or driving cattle to market. It was often the only home they knew, and their fellow cowboys were family. The cook who fed them on the trail also fed them here. Some smaller ranches had living quarters for their cowboys, but they all took their meals together.

It was no vacation; the ranch offered its share of backbreaking work. The cowboys broke horses, mended fences, and did a multitude of other ranch-related jobs.

Even though they worked hard on the ranch, they did have some time to participate in fun events. Sometimes there were rodeos where neighboring ranch owners pitted their best cowboys against each other. If the ranch wasn't too remote, the cowboys living there had access to a town, church, and other social activities. Some places had dances, picnics, and streams to fish in.

While the cowboys all stayed under one room with multiple bunks, the boss's house was much nicer. It tended to be a more typical house with a dining room, bedrooms, a parlor, an office, and other rooms. The size of the boss's house was indicative of the size of the ranch itself. The more stock and hired hands there were, the larger the rancher's house was.

The rancher's wife normally did the cooking, but some women were fortunate enough to have a cook working for them in the ranch house. The boss often had a family and children growing up on cattle ranches and interacting with the hired hands.

Special events like Thanksgiving and Christmas may have been the few times when the cowboys were invited to events at the "big house."

Cattle ranches evolved during the latter part of the nineteenth century and into the twentieth century. The *Topeka Daily State Journal* ran a story in 1918 comparing the ranch of the mid-1800s to the current ones. The article called "A Twentieth-Century Ranch" stated:

The modern western cattle-ranch is a curious combination of the up-to-date and the primitive, of last-century romance and scientific practicality. The cattle-ranch of western fiction has vanished from everywhere but the movie-screen; the traditional cowboy, who hardly equaled his prototype in melodrama even in his prime, is nowhere to be found now. In his place is a capable individual who handles a bronco and a Ford with equal nonchalance, drives a mule or a motor truck and trailer with about the same outlay of profanity. A visit to a big southwestern ranch, where the open range is making its last stand against the barb-wire fence and the homesteader, gives an interesting picture of the cattle business up to date. Under the old system of working cattle, with ten or twelve cowpunchers and a chuck-wagon assigned to each division of the enormous estate, each man with a "string" of eight or nine ponies, it would have required sixty men and four or five hundred horses to take care of the cattle. The actual crew for the whole ranch is only fourteen men. The bulk of the land in this ranch lies in low, rolling hills sparsely foliated with fragrant cedar bushes. An elaborate system of roads has been laid out, radiating from the central ranch house. One of the most important cogs in the ranch machinery is a big road scraper pulled by a motor truck. Each of the cow punchers has a light automobile assigned to him for his own use, and he has to be conversant with carburetor troubles as he is with the beaves, and similar equine diseases. By the use of the motors, each man multiplies his efficiency about ten times. On the old, great ranches, a cowboy spent a large part of his life in getting from place to place. It might be a two-day ride from the ranch-house to the front gate. The auto practically eliminates distance. No sight could possibly be more typical of the modern West, or more shocking to the romanticist who sees his ideal cowboy mounted on a champing cayuse than that of a soberly garbed, high-hatted man in shirt-sleeves chasing a bunch of yearlings down a canyon by honking madly on the siren of his Ford.

Children on the Ranch

Agnes Morley Cleaveland grew up on a ranch in New Mexico toward the end of the nineteenth century. She was born in 1874 in Cimarron, but later moved with her family to Magdalena.

Cleaveland's 1941 book, *No Life for a Lady*, describes her life on the ranch. She talked about all her experiences, including what she ate. Agnes wrote about the luxuries that were occasionally available on her rural ranch. Many pioneers learned how to "eat off the land" and use substitutions for well-known recipes. Sometimes they ate health foods without even knowing it. Agnes wrote, "Of course we were always casting about for some little epicurean luxury, so in early spring we often has lamb's-quarter greens and occasionally sheep sorrel pie . . . The acid-sweet of a sheep sorrel makes a delectable pie, but it takes so much of the short-stemmed clover-leaf-shaped plant that only when all hands gathered sheep sorrel would we hope for the luxury of a pie." Oddly enough, sheep sorrel is high in antioxidants and vitamin C, and has been proven to cure cancer in some cases. But too much can cause kidney stones and send you running to the outhouse.

Agnes was also familiar with the lemon pie substitute called vinegar pie, "Usually we had to be content with vinegar pie. The recipe for vinegar pie was as follows: Make a flour and vinegar base, seasoned with sugar, and cook until it thickens. It might be simpler to state the recipe, Make a good quality paperhanger's paste and season to taste. But make no mistake, it's good!"

She wrote that the main dessert on the ranch was bread and lick, which is syrup, like molasses, honey, or sorghum, to name a few. The foods she remembered from the ranch were similar to chuck wagon grub. They are meat, potatoes dug fresh, beans and sowbelly (salt pork), and dried fruit. She added, "bread, a term which meant sour-dough biscuit almost exclusively . . . and for a touch of luxury, 'canned goods.' Eggs? Not regularly. Too many predatory animals to make chicken-raising much more than a series of minor tragedies."

Agnes was nice enough to describe jerky and how to make it, "When a beef has been butchered . . . and you know that even what is left will spoil before it can be eaten, take this surplus, cut into long strips, salt, and hang over the clothesline. Don't get excited about the flies. It will dry so rapidly the flies will become discouraged. In a couple of days it will [be] as hard as a cedar chip. . . . To serve, eat as is, or throw onto hot coals and roast, or, if time is no object, pound into a fibrous pulp, fry, and cover with milk gravy—and don't envy a city slicker at his banquet table." She also talked about how they enjoyed coffee with doughnuts made of sourdough, which they served to company. They made applesauce with dried apples and one of Agnes's favorites was sliced bread with butter and brown sugar on top.

Even though Agnes was a lady, she didn't let the Victorian way of life interfere with how she lived on the ranch. She wrote, "We never forbade card-playing on our place in the long winter evenings. We tried to make it as tolerable as possible . . . It was a nice problem, this fine line between entertainment and vice . . . I thought to solve it the one winter I stayed home; I would play cards with the boys! We'd play in our dining room and not in the bunkhouse, one sociable family! Meekly they came. I was bubbling good will. We'd play poker for beans!"

DRIED BEEF

SERVES 2–4

 4 ounces dehydrated beef
 2 tablespoons butter
 2 tablespoons flour
 2 cups milk
 Pepper to taste

Chop the beef into bite-size pieces and set aside.

Melt the butter in a medium saucepan over low heat.

Whisk in the flour and cook for 1–2 minutes.

Add the milk and stir until thick.

Add the beef and stir.

Add pepper to taste and serve over toast or mashed potatoes.

RECIPE ADAPTED BY THE AUTHOR BASED ON THE PRECEDING STORY.

VINEGAR PIE

MAKES 1 PIE

 1 cup brown sugar
 1 cup water
 ½ cup cider vinegar
 2 tablespoons butter
 ½ cup flour
 ¼ cup water
 Piecrust

Combine the sugar, water, and vinegar, and bring to a boil.

Add the butter and stir until it melts. Remove from the heat and allow to cool for about 15 minutes.

Mix the flour and water and beat until the mixture is smooth.

Take ¼ cup of the sugar mixture, add it to the flour slurry, and quickly stir.

Slowly add the flour mixture to the sugar pot, and quickly stir.

Return the mixture to the heat and cook over medium-high heat until it becomes thick.

Pour the filling into the piecrust-lined pan.

Bake at 450°F for 10 minutes, then reduce heat to 350°F and bake about 25 minutes more.

RECIPE ADAPTED BY THE AUTHOR BASED ON THE PRECEDING STORY.

MASHED POTATOES

This recipe was called "Potato Snow" in Omaha's *Daily World* newspaper in 1886.

SERVES 4–6

    1 teaspoon salt
    6–8 large potatoes
    3 tablespoons butter
    ½ cup milk
    Salt and pepper to taste

Add a teaspoon of salt to a large pot of water and bring to boil over high heat.

Peel and chop potatoes and add to the water. Simmer until a fork easily pierces through, about 15 minutes.

Drain and return the potatoes to the pot.

Add the butter and milk to the potatoes, and mash.

Season with salt and pepper.

RECIPE ADAPTED FROM THE *OMAHA DAILY WORLD*, DECEMBER 4, 1886.

CREAMED POTATOES AU GRATIN

SERVES 4–6

    6 medium potatoes
    1 cup cream
    ½ cup milk
    1 tablespoon butter
    1 teaspoon salt
    Pepper to taste
    1 cup cheddar cheese, grated
    ½ cup bread crumbs

Bring a pot of water to boil over high heat.

Peel and dice the potatoes and add to the water. Cook until just tender—about 15 minutes. Drain.

Place the cream, milk, butter, salt, and pepper into the pot. Add the cooked potatoes and bring to a boil.

Butter a baking dish big enough to hold 2 layers of the potatoes. Place half the potatoes in the dish and sprinkle with half the cheese and breadcrumbs.

Add the remaining potatoes and sprinkle with the remaining cheese and breadcrumbs.

Bake at 400°F for about 15 minutes or until the top is bubbling.

RECIPE ADAPTED FROM LAS CRUCES, NEW MEXICO'S *INDEPENDENT DEMOCRAT*, MARCH 26, 1896.

SOURDOUGH DOUGHNUTS

MAKES ABOUT A DOZEN

   3 tablespoons butter or lard, melted
   ½ cup white sugar
   2 eggs, beaten
   1 cup Sourdough Starter
   ½ cup milk
   2–3 cups all-purpose flour
   ½ teaspoon baking soda
   ½ teaspoon nutmeg
   ½ teaspoon salt
   4 cups vegetable oil (for frying)

In a large mixing bowl, combine butter, sugar, eggs, starter, and milk.

In a separate bowl, mix together 2½ cups flour, baking soda, nutmeg, and salt.

Add flour mixture into the starter mixture and stir until blended. If dough seems too wet, then add the extra flour in ¼-cup increments.

Roll out dough on a floured surface to ½-inch thickness.

Cut dough with a doughnut cutter and place on a greased cookie sheet. Cover and let rest for 1 hour.

About 10 minutes before frying, heat the oil in a deep stockpot to 375°F.

Gently place each doughnut into the hot oil and cook until golden brown on one side, and then turn over and cook until golden.

Place fried doughnuts on paper towels and sprinkle them with your favorite toppings, such as cinnamon and sugar, or powdered sugar.

RECIPE ADAPTED FROM TEXAS'S *DENISON DAILY NEWS*, JANUARY 13, 1878.

APPLESAUCE

The original recipe states, "Make a syrup of equal parts water and molasses or brown sugar (white is nicer, of course)."

MAKES ABOUT 2 QUARTS

   7–10 tart, firm apples
   ½ cup white or brown sugar
   1 cup water

Core, quarter, and peel the apples.

Place in a heavy saucepan and add the sugar and water.

Bring to a boil over high heat and then reduce to low heat.

Cook for 30–45 minutes or until the apples are soft enough to mash.

Mash and serve warm or cold.

RECIPE ADAPTED FROM THE *KANSAS HOME COOK BOOK*, 1874.

Comfortable

"I joined up with the 'Half Circle J,' so named because of the brand . . . The outfit was owned by Hardy Watson and his camp was located near Shamrock, Wheeler Co., Texas. The 'Half Circle J' outfit run better than 15000 head of cattle and 400 head of horses. There was a crew of seven hands besides the two sons of Watson. Jim Watson was the top-screw and Jack was the belly-cheater," wrote cowboy Luther Hart. "The cattle grazed on a fenced range and were Herefords and blackpolls. We lived well while on the home ranch. The chuck was the best and we had plenty variety of well-cooked grub. As usual on a cow outfit, beef was the main meat dish, but Watson backed that up with lots of canned vegetables and there was always something to satisfy our sweet tooth."

Colorado cowboy George Stiers recalled his bunkhouse at the Brand Ranch owned by the Eddy brothers near Selidell: "We had a large bunkhouse to sleep in when not out on the range too far to get in. There was a big shed with long tables where we sit down to line our flue. Pat Lawson was the chief cook and a good belly cheater, who spent years with the outfit. He always went with the chuck-wagon and left his helpers at the main joint. That was a nice country to work in during the summer, but the winters often took the silver out of your cloud. Bud McDonald was the top-screw and a square shooter, which helped in a time of a bad spell of weather. He would not ask us waddies to go when he would not. He always was with us in times of trouble. When a cold spell of weather hit he would send canteens of hot, thick, black coffee to the night riders. Curley Lawson would stay up all night fix'ng coffee when a real bad spell was a busting. When the riders came in off their shifts there was a snack and all the hot coffee one wanted waiting."

Theodore Roosevelt's Elkhorn Ranch

America's twenty-sixth president was a cattle rancher in the late 1800s, and he also went on roundups. After the tragic deaths of both his wife and mother on Valentine's Day in 1884, he located his Elkhorn Ranch in the Badlands of South Dakota. He wrote, "A ranchman's life is certainly a very pleasant one, albeit generally varied with plenty of hardship and anxiety. Although occasionally he passes days of severe toil,—for example, if he goes on the round-up he works as hard as any of his men,—yet he no longer has to undergo the monotonous drudgery attendant upon the tasks of the cowboy or of the apprentice in the business. His fare is simple; but, if he chooses, it is good enough. Many ranches are provided with nothing at all but salt pork, canned goods, and bread; indeed, it is a curious fact that in traveling through the cow country it is often impossible to get any milk or butter; but this is only because the owners or managers are too lazy to take enough trouble to insure their own comfort. We ourselves always keep up two or three cows, choosing such as are naturally tame, and so we invariably have plenty of milk and, when there is time for churning, a good deal of butter. We also keep hens, which, in spite of the damaging inroads of hawks, bob-cats, and foxes, supply us with eggs, and in time of need, when our rifles have failed to keep us in game, with stewed, roast, or fried chicken also. From our garden we get potatoes, and unless drought, frost, or grasshoppers interfere (which they do about every second year), other vegetables as well. For fresh meat we depend chiefly upon our prowess as hunters." He remained on his ranch until the brutal winter of 1886–1887 wiped out his entire herd of cattle. He then returned to New York, and well, the rest is history.

STEWED CHICKEN

SERVES 4-6

   3 pounds chicken, boneless breasts and thighs
   6 cups water
   Salt and freshly ground pepper
   4-6 large potatoes, peeled and cubed
   2 cups light cream
   ½ cup flour
   2 tablespoons butter

Place the chicken, water, 1 teaspoon salt, and pepper to taste in a large stockpot.

Bring to a boil, cook for 15 minutes, and then add the potatoes.

Cook another 15 minutes or until chicken is done.

Remove chicken and potatoes from the pot and reserve the broth.

Shred the chicken into small pieces and set aside.

Heat the reserved broth over medium heat.

Combine the light cream and flour together in a bowl, and stir to remove any lumps.

Whisk this and the butter into the chicken broth and taste for seasoning. Add salt and pepper if needed.

Cook over medium-low heat until thickened—about 20 minutes.

Add the chicken and heat through.

RECIPE ADAPTED FROM IOWA'S *SIOUX CITY JOURNAL*, JUNE 9, 1895.

FRIED CHICKEN

SERVES 4–6

  1 (3-pound) chicken, cut up
  Water
  Salt
  1½ cups flour
  ½ teaspoon freshly ground pepper
  2 eggs
  2 cups bread crumbs
  Lard and/or butter, enough to cover chicken
    for frying

Place the chicken in a bowl and cover with water. Add 2 tablespoons salt and soak for 2 hours.

Drain and pat completely dry.

Place the flour, 1 teaspoon salt, and pepper in shallow bowl.

Beat the eggs in a small bowl and place the bread crumbs in a bag or deep bowl.

Coat each piece of chicken with the flour, then dip each in egg, and then in the breadcrumbs.

Place the lard and/or butter in a large frying pan or dutch oven (cast iron is best) and heat over medium-high heat.

Gently place the chicken in the oil, using tongs. The oil should bubble immediately after the chicken is added. Slowly add the chicken so the temperature does not drop, and work in batches to avoid overcrowding.

Fry the chicken until golden brown, turning once, 10–20 minutes, depending on the size of the pieces.

Check for doneness by piercing the meat; the juices should run clear.

When done, place the chicken on paper towels or a wire rack. Salt to taste.

Place the cooked chicken in a 180°F oven to keep warm while the other pieces are being cooked.

Caution: Do not get water anywhere near the hot oil because it will cause the oil to explode.

RECIPE ADAPTED FROM THE OMAHA, NEBRASKA, *WORLD-HERALD*, JULY 16, 1899.

POTATOES AND CREAM

SERVES 4–6

  4–6 large potatoes
  ½ teaspoon salt
  6 tablespoons butter
  Salt and pepper to taste
  1 cup cream

Peel and dice the potatoes.

Add salt to a pot of water and bring to a boil over high heat.

Add the potatoes and cook just until tender— about 20 minutes. Drain.

Place cooked potatoes in a buttered baking dish and dot with butter.

Add the salt, pepper, and cream.

Bake uncovered at 350°F for about 10 minutes or until the butter melts.

RECIPE ADAPTED FROM SOUTH DAKOTA'S *ABERDEEN NEWS*, FEBRUARY 26, 1886.

Roosevelt Returns to the West

In 1903 President Roosevelt returned to the West and was treated to some good old-fashioned chuck wagon grub. The *Valentine Democrat* in Lincoln, Nebraska, ran an interview with the man who cooked for the president while in Hugo, Colorado. Jack Keppel was a retired cookie, but was selected for this job because of his expertise. He recalled, "I was very proud . . . when the Lincoln County Cattle Grower's Association selected me to take charge of the cooking of the cowboy breakfast which we had determined to serve to President Roosevelt . . . John (Heyman) and I then made twelve gallons of coffee in three big pots and got the French fried potatoes ready. The next thing was to make the biscuits and put them in the dutch oven. It's quite a job to make good biscuits, and you bet I was very particular with these . . . When the President's train was in sight we got pretty excited around that campfire, I can tell you. I had picked out a big T-bone steak, the finest one I ever saw, for the President. As the train was slowing up I nodded to John Heyman, my assistant, to drop the big steak on the hot surface of the dutch oven, which was on the rack, and heated up just about right. By the time the biscuits were done to a turn and everything was ready . . . Well, I have cooked many a steak, but I was certainly more proud of that one than any I ever turned out. It was a regular 'beaut' and when Teddy cut into it and munched the first mouthful and I saw the tickled expressions of his face I was so proud—well, I just had to swing my hat and holler."

The president picked up one of Keppel's browned rolls and was reported to have said, "That's the dutch oven kind—that is . . . that is the proper thing."

A Cowboy's Ball

In 1886 a *Chicago Tribune* newspaper correspondent attended a ranch ball in North Dakota and wrote a story about what he saw. He began,

When all had arrived I should judge there were about fifty cowboys present and about fifteen ladies. Some little time was spent in thawing out and then the fun began. Let no Eastern tenderfoot imagine that a cowboy goes to a ball with a six-shooter stuck in each boot and a butcher knife like an ice-saw protruding from the back of his neck. While there were lots of noise and fun going on, which at times drowned out the two left-handed fiddlers who were sawing away for dear life. I did not hear a word or see an act that might not have been seen in an Eastern ballroom, where only swallow-tail coats and white kid gloves could enter. From all I could see the programme of dances was about the same as that adopted by the Arizona or Texas cowboys at their dances. A recent arrival from the South had brought it up and it was tacked to the wall where everybody could see it. It ran as follows:

Grand Circle Round-up March
Horse-Hunters' Quadrille
Catch Horse Waltz
Saddle-up Lancers
Broncho Racket
Captain's Quadrille
Circular Gallop
Cut-out Schottische
Branding Quadrille
Cow and Calf Racket

My friend, at whose invitation I was present, seeing me stand an idle spectator, shouted as he whirled by, "Git a partner and pitch in!" But I left them to their innocent, happy enjoyment, and remained a wall-flower throughout the balance of the evening. When the gay revelers had danced unremittingly until 1 a.m., a halt was called and supper announced. The supper was spread in a large tent at the back of the main building, and this canvas house was made comfortable and pleasant by the aid of a large stove. There were oysters, turkey, venison, and all manners of canned goods, coffee, and cigars in abundance, but not one drop of whiskey or spirituous drinks of any kind. When supper was finished the order came for, "on with the dance," and so it was kept up until morning. It was a revelation to me, this life at a cattle ranch in the dead of winter, and I departed much pleased with my visit.

FRIED OYSTERS

MAKES 12

> 2 eggs
> 1 teaspoon salt
> ⅛ teaspoon cayenne pepper
> 1 cup flour
> 1 cup fine bread or cracker crumbs
> 1 dozen oysters
> Oil for frying

Beat eggs in a small mixing bowl. Add salt and pepper.

Place the flour and crumbs in separate shallow dishes.

Dip the oysters, 1 at a time, in the flour, then in the eggs, and finally in the crumbs.

Gently place the oysters into hot oil.

Fry until golden; about 2 minutes on each side.

Remove and drain on a paper towel.

RECIPE ADAPTED FROM NORTH DAKOTA'S *BISMARCK DAILY TRIBUNE*, JANUARY 29, 1892.

William S. "Two Gun Bill" Hart, the Cowboy Actor

Cowboy actor William S. Hart started his career as a stage actor and transitioned to movies when he was fifty. Within a few years, he became one of the most popular and successful actors in the world. He was beloved by countless fans, including President Woodrow Wilson. He acted in over forty-five full-length movies, including *Tumbleweeds* and *Two Gun Bill*.

Hart's experiences as a youth may account for his success: "The first fifteen years of my life were spent in the Dakota Territory. The great West mothered me during the shaping of my boyhood ambitions and ideals. Therefore, I know by personal experience much of the actual life of our frontier days." By 1920 Hart had become a celebrated western-movie actor, and he also wrote a newspaper column called Campfire Stories. His stories were aimed at the young boys who wrote him letters inquiring about his Wild West adventures.

Story 9 covered the day-to-day life of a cowboy and some of the costs associated with the job. He wrote, "It is sure going to surprise you boys to know that it costs more for a cowboy to dress than it does this city man. Of course, the city man's wardrobe may cost more because he indulges in many suits and shirts and shoes, but article for article, the cowboy's outfit is a great deal more costly. And, remember, each article of the puncher's outfit is as necessary as it may be decorative.

"For instance, cowboys wear big Stetson hats for protection against the weather. The big western hat shades a man's eyes from the sun, or it keeps the rain from beating on the face. There are three kinds of Stetson hats: felt, velour and beaver. The last named is the costliest. Today a cowboy beaver hat costs from $35 to $100 and sometimes more. Velour hats run anywhere from $15 to $50 in price, and felts from $5 to $25. Even in this day of outrageous prices city men do not pay as much money for their hats. The hat band may be either hair or beaded, and of course, it has no particular use except for what it is intended. Most 'tenderfeet' believe that the big bandana silk handkerchiefs that the cowboys wear around their necks are for show. You will no doubt be surprised to know that when a cowboy is riding the range he finds these 'mufflers' absolutely necessary, since it is pulled up over the nose and mouth for protection against the choking dust.

"The most durable and serviceable shirts for punchers are flannel shirts. And yet, boys, it doesn't follow that the silk shirts you have seen cowboys wear are just for show. It is ornaments. However, when working on the ranch a puncher sticks to plain chaps. High-heeled boots are one of the most important essentials of a puncher's outfit. Maybe they aren't designed to walk in, but whoever heard of a real cowboy who wanted to walk?

"Instead, they keep a puncher's feet from slipping out of the stirrups while working. The best boots are made of calfskin. Mine have morocco leather tops and a little fancy stitching on them. The woolen sash which is worn about the waist may look like fancy trimmings, but it is used instead of a leather belt. It is much more comfortable, and besides, it can be used to hog-tie young calves instead of carrying an extra rope."

Hart often played the role of a villain, and Story 13, which appeared on September 4, 1920, addressed what a real cowboy and ranch life were like. He penned, "First of all boys, a ranch in the west is always called an 'outfit.' Many outfits are known by their brands, such as the Circle Diamond . . . Work on the old-time ranch was done solely by the men and horses. Don't ever get the idea that the cowboy was a 'bad man,' who went around shooting up everybody who crossed him. In the last twenty years a real cowboy hardly ever 'packed' a six-gun, tho of course every man owned a six-shooter for protection in traversing the trails in the open country. As a class of men, cowboys are and always have been hard-working men, with a strict sense of right and wrong . . . Their deep respect for women has always been a 'law of the west'."

After setting his young readers right on the makeup of a real cowboy, Hart wrote about the chuck wagon: "Chuckwagon seems to interest you boys—and well it may, because it carries the food for the cowboys. First I will explain that when the actual cow-work on a ranch is on, such as rounding up the cattle, branding, and so forth, it is done by what is known as the 'wagon outfit.' This consists of the chuckwagon and the 'bedwagon.' In the former is carried the food, which is cooked over an open fire from the back of the wagon. 'Chuck' consists of the best food obtainable on the ranch, such as beef, beans, potatoes, cornbread

The Belle Fouche Ranch in Sturgis, Dakota Territory, ca. 1887. *Courtesy Library of Congress*

and other staples. And boys, there is no meal in the best restaurant in the world that tastes as good as 'chuck' out in the open after hours of man's work. I always take a chuckwagon with me on location while producing motion pictures, and when visitors come out in the dessert or the mountain, as the case may be to see us work, they never fail to go away singing the praises of 'chuck' and the camp cook.

"By the way, boys, the cowboy cook is the monarch of the chuckwagon. Woe to the puncher who gets the cook 'riled' by fooling around with the wagon because he may be hauled into 'kangaroo court' after the day's work is done and punished. You can well understand how important a good cook is to an outfit of hard-working men far away from civilization, out on the open range. Such life makes men hungry, and it behooves everybody in an outfit to keep off the cook's toes. There is an old saying on the ranches, 'techy as a cook,' which means that cooks are considered somewhat temperamental. But don't get the idea that cooks on the range are just cooks. Of course they don't do anything else but cook, but in most cases are just as good cowboys as cooks, and in many cases better cowboys."

Dog Face

The cookie at the CA Bar Ranch in Colorado County, Texas, was simply called, Dog Face. Young cowboy Henry Young recalled, "The CA Bar grazed critters over about 60 sections of land, running around 10,000 head. There were 15 steady hands, and extra hands were hired during branding season. No hands lived in a log ranch house. The house where the hands lived was called the 'ranch house' and the owner's home the 'ranch home,' or the 'Bull's ranch.' In the ranch house we slept on bunks and we waddies had to take care of our dump. We had our own cookie. 'Dog Face' is the only name, I recall, we had for him. He was a good cook and made dandy sour-dough bread, was a good bean cook, too. Lots of times he fixed us bean-hole beans, that is, beans cooked in a hole. Dog Face would dig a hole in the ground, line the hole with stone, then build a fire in the hole and keep it burning for several hours. Those stones would get piping hot, then the hole was ready for the beans. He put the beans into an iron kettle, with a tight cover, set it in the hole and covered it with sand. There they would be left for several hours. He seasoned the whistleberries with bacon and molasses. I am telling you, those beans were fitting to eat. Beef, beans, a few canned vegetables and dried fruit was the chief chuck on which we lived. Half of the time we ate the chuck sitting on our haunches behind the chuck wagon."

Cowboys often "squatted" while they ate their meals, since they wore spurs. Photo ca. 1905; *Courtesy Library of Congress*

Bunkhouse Cookie

Ernest Spann and his wife Eva worked on the HF Ranch in 1900. He recalled, "I married when I was 17 years old, then was put to calculating on getting a job. I got wind of a job for a cowhand and a cookie on the 'HF' outfit, owned by Hamp Franchee, located in Baylor County, 15 miles south of Seymour. Eva, my wife, and I started for the ranch each straddled on a bronco and dragged out to HF ranch. We were taken on, she as cookie and I as a cowhand. That was in 1900 and we stayed with the outfit four years. My wife had, on the average, fifteen hands to fix chuck for. Sometimes the number would be as low as eight and at times high as twenty. During the [?] season the number of waddies would be just enough to attend to the general work, but during branding season and when there was a lot of shipping the number of hands would be up to twenty. We had the best of everything to eat and did most of our flue lining in the cook shack. Only during branding seasons, occasionally, we used the chuck wagon. My wife was ordered to feed the hands well and that she did. Of course, there were no fancy dishes fixed, but plenty of good solid food of all kinds needed, including chuck for the sweet tooth."

Vittles on the Ranch

George Martin worked on the RR Ranch in Denton County, Texas, and remembered his life there. "Our chuck run strong to beef and beans. The beef was not considered as costing anything, because the country was full of cattle and when some beef was wanted a waddie would rope a fat yearling and never look at the brand. What was a fact, generally the best looking yearling carried the brand of some other ranch. Besides beef, we would have wild game, whenever the cookie took the notion, or one of the waddies would decide to vary the meat deal, they would go out and shoot some game. Our bread was biscuits, sourdough, or corn-pone. We had some vegetables which came in the can, dried fruit and all the black coffee we [called?] for. The cookie would regularly fix up something for our sweet tooth, such as fried pies made from dried fruit, pudding of some sort and once in a while a cake."

APRICOT FRIED PIES

MAKES 6 PIES (INDIVIDUAL SERVINGS)

6 ounces dried apricots or cherries
¾ cup sugar
1 piecrust recipe (See recipe in chapter 2.)
Oil for frying

Place dried fruit in a medium saucepan and add enough water just to cover. Bring to a boil over high heat and cook until the fruit is tender and the water has evaporated.

Add the sugar and cook for another 2–3 minutes.

Remove from the heat and mash. Cool.

Roll out piecrust to ¼-inch thickness and then cut into 6-inch circles or whatever size is desired.

Place a tablespoon of the fruit on one side of the piecrust.

Moisten the circle with water and fold it in half. Use a fork to seal the edges.

Add enough oil to a large stockpot to come up ½ inch.

Heat over medium-high heat. Test the oil by adding a small piece of leftover piecrust. If it bubbles, then the oil is ready.

Gently add the pies, 3 at a time, with tongs.

Cook for about 2 minutes on one side, and then turn over and cook until golden.

Drain on paper towels.

Caution: Filling will be hot.

RECIPE ADAPTED FROM *SCAMMELL'S CYCLOPEDIA OF VALUABLE RECEIPTS*, 1897.

ROAST QUAIL

SERVES 4

4 quail
8 tablespoons butter
½ cup flour
Salt and pepper to taste
4 bacon slices

Wash the quail inside and out and pat dry.

Place 2 tablespoons of butter inside each quail.

Combine flour, salt, and pepper in a shallow pan.

Dredge the birds in the flour to coat evenly.

Wrap a slice of bacon over each quail.

Place in a roasting pan and bake uncovered at 350°F for 25 minutes or until done. Remove bacon before slicing.

Note: If you can't get quail in your area, substitute capons or Cornish game hens.

RECIPE ADAPTED FROM *SCAMMELL'S CYCLOPEDIA OF VALUABLE RECEIPTS*, 1897.

CORN PONE

SERVES 6–8

    ¼ cup canola oil
    1½ cups cornmeal
    ½ cup sugar
    ½ teaspoon salt
    1 teaspoon baking soda
    1⅓ cups buttermilk
    2 eggs

Preheat the oven to 425°F.

Pour the oil into a 9-inch, cast-iron frying pan and place in the oven for 10 minutes.

Combine the dry ingredients in a large bowl.

Place buttermilk and eggs in a small bowl and beat well.

Add the eggs and milk to the dry ingredients and stir until just blended.

Take the pan out of the oven and swirl the oil to coat the pan.

Pour the mixture into the hot frying pan and place back in the oven.

Bake for 20–25 minutes or until a toothpick inserted into the center comes out clean.

Remove the pan from the oven and shake the pan to loosen the corn pone. Turn out onto a plate and serve warm.

RECIPE ADAPTED FROM THE OMAHA, NEBRASKA, *WORLD-HERALD*, APRIL 9, 1899.

BREAD PUDDING

SERVES 6–8

    12 slices day-old baguette, cut into ¾-inch cubes
    ½ stick butter, melted
    4 cups milk
    4 eggs, beaten
    ½ teaspoon salt
    1 cup light brown sugar
    ½ grated nutmeg (about ½ teaspoon)
    ½ pound currants or raisins, optional
    1 teaspoon vanilla (suggested, but not in original recipe)
    ½ teaspoon cinnamon (suggested, but not in original recipe)

Cut the bread into cubes and place in bowl.

Add the butter and stir to combine.

Add all the remaining ingredients and mix well. Allow to sit until the bread is soaked with the milk, about 20 minutes.

Pour into a buttered 9 x 12-inch pan, and bake at 350°F for about 45 minutes.

Allow to sit and cool before serving.

RECIPE ADAPTED FROM THE *FREDERICKSBURG* (TEXAS) *HOME KITCHEN COOK BOOK*, 1916.

Montana Cowboys

A Montana cowboy recalled his days on the Crazy D Ranch in the late 1800s. At the age of thirteen, George Flanders started his career as a cowboy at a cattle ranch owned by C. H. and V. H. Phenny, whose brand was the Crazy D. Of the six years he remained with the Crazy D ranch, he recalled, "The ranch was located 57 miles West of Helena, Mont. At that time about 12 houses was all the building the town had. We had to go there for our mail and supplies, that trip was made once a month. In that 57 miles there was no sign of any dwelling. Our camp shelter was made out of gumbo mud and poles. Our chuck consisted of Beef, buffalo, deer, elk, prairie-hens and other game. Beans and bread with some canned vegetables backed up the meat. I don't want to forget the black coffee, of that we had all we cared to drink. Our cook was Fanny Carter. Aunt Fanny we called her and she was the wife of Bill Carter, the top-screw and a good foreman, too."

VENISON STEAK

SERVES 4–6

1 tablespoon butter
1 tablespoon flour
½ cup beef broth
½ cup currant jelly

4–6 (½-inch-thick) venison steaks
Salt and pepper to taste
Butter or bacon grease

For the sauce

Melt the butter in a medium saucepan over medium heat.

Add the flour and cook for 1 minute.

Add the broth and cook for another 2 minutes and then add the jelly.

Stir until blended and remove from heat.

For the meat

Rub the steaks with butter and salt and pepper to taste.

Heat a frying pan or grill to high.

Place the steaks on the grill, and sear them uncovered for 1–2 minutes on one side for medium rare. Do not press or move the steaks.

After desired cooking time is reached, flip the steaks and grill for 2 minutes uncovered.

Turn the heat to low and cover for another 2 minutes.

Pour sauce over the steaks and serve.

RECIPE ADAPTED FROM THE *KANSAS HOME COOK BOOK*, 1874

ELK STEAK

SERVES 4–6

4–6 (1-inch-thick) elk steaks
Butter
Salt and pepper to taste
8 slices bacon

Rub the steaks with butter and salt and pepper to taste.

Heat a frying pan to high.

Place the steaks in the frying pan and lay enough bacon to cover the top.

Sear the steaks uncovered for 2 minutes on one side for medium rare. Do not press or move the steaks.

After desired cooking time is reached, flip the steaks and cook for 2 minutes uncovered.

Allow steaks to rest for 5 minutes before serving.

RECIPE ADAPTED FROM IOWA'S *SIOUX CITY JOURNAL*, MAY 13, 1895.

SALMI OF PRAIRIE HENS (CHICKEN STEW)

SERVES 4–6

2 tablespoons butter or bacon fat
2 tablespoons flour
2 cups cooked chicken
4 cups chicken stock
½ teaspoon salt
Freshly ground pepper to taste
½ lemon, juiced
¼ cup onion, diced
½ teaspoon turmeric
1 teaspoon fresh chopped parsley
½ teaspoon sage and marjoram

Melt the butter in a large dutch oven or stockpot over medium heat.

Add the flour and cook for 1 minute.

Add the remaining ingredients, bring the pot to a boil, and then simmer for 30 minutes.

Serve over rice or toasted bread and peas.

RECIPE ADAPTED FROM ST. LOUIS, MISSOURI'S *REPUBLIC*, OCTOBER 23, 1892.

Cowboy Fishing

G. W. Mills moved to Texas with his father in 1872 and settled near Lockhart, Texas. When he was seventeen he went to work at M. A. Withers, James R. Withers, and Gus Withers's ranch known as the Olmas Ranch, about four miles from his home.

Part of James's obituary provides a time frame. It read, "Mr. Withers came to La Salle County in 1885 from Lockhart, and engaged in the ranch business. Associated with him were his uncle M. A. Withers, and brother, Gus Withers. The latter died several years ago. In the early days they operated what was known as the Olmas Ranch, now the Dobie ranch. In 1895 Mr. Withers located on and began the improvement of the ranch where he died."

Mills recalled, "I think it would be of interest to the reader to have some idea of the appearance of that ranch as it appeared to me, then a mere lad. It was located on a little flowing stream known as Clear Fork and abundantly fed by many springs. This creek was fringed with timber, pecan, walnut, elm, hackberry and wild plum on either bank, and dipping into its crystal waters were the weeping willows. The creek abounded with an abundance of fish, such as bass, channel cat and the silver perch. The old ranch house stood back about three hundred yards east of the creek, on the summit of a gradual sloping hillside, which commanded a view of the beautiful stretch of valley country roundabout and where it was swept by the gentle southern breeze. About one hundred and fifty yards from the house were the corrals, covering about four acres of ground, and these corrals were divided into various pens, in which we 'rounded up' from time to time the great herds for marking and branding."

FRIED BASS

SERVES 4–6

> 2 eggs, beaten
> 1 cup cracker meal or fine bread crumbs
> 1 pound bass fillets
> Salt and pepper to taste
> ¼ cup oil for frying

Place eggs in a bowl and cracker meal in another.

Salt and pepper the fillets and then dip in egg and then cracker meal.

In a large frying pan, heat the oil over medium-high heat.

Gently add fillets to pan, and cook 5 minutes on each side or until fish flakes easily when tested with a fork.

Sprinkle with a little more salt and pepper to taste.

RECIPE ADAPTED FROM THE *OMAHA DAILY WORLD*, APRIL 23, 1887.

FRIED CATFISH

SERVES 4–6

- 3 eggs
- ½ teaspoon salt
- ¼ teaspoon freshly ground pepper
- 1 teaspoon Worcestershire sauce
- 1 cup cornmeal
- 1 pound (1-inch-thick) catfish fillets
- ¼ cup oil for frying

Beat the eggs in a small bowl and add the salt, pepper, and Worcestershire sauce.

Place cornmeal in a separate bowl.

Dip the fillets into the eggs and then into the cornmeal.

Heat the oil in a frying pan over medium heat and gently add the fillets.

Cook 4–8 minutes, turning once, until fish flakes easily with fork and is brown on both sides.

Drain on paper towels.

RECIPE ADAPTED FROM *SCAMMELL'S CYCLOPEDIA OF VALUABLE RECEIPTS*, 1897.

From a Rancher's View

Herbert Hilsop and Walter Vail bought Edward Nye Fish's ranch in 1876. The ranch was located between Tucson and Sonoita. Herbert was an Englishman and acted as the cook for the ranch for a while. He and Walter went on a week-long scouting mission to the Fish ranch in July. They wanted to experience the ranch before they bought it. By September they would purchase the ranch from Fish and rename it Empire.

On July 24, 1876, Herbert wrote to his sister Amy, "The third day I was appointed cook and so while they were out in the morning herding, I was making bread and preparing dinner. It was grand fun, if anyone could have seen me making bread. I put it in the bake pot (here they bake it in pots, having no ovens) and my fire was too hot and began to raise it too quickly and when I thought it was nicely done I took it out but found on cutting it open it was in the same condition in the middle as when I put it in so I cut it in quarters and baked it separately very well indeed. As I had some time to spare before their return, I thought I would make some custard which was thoroughly appreciated and very nice indeed though I say it myself."

Once they got settled at the Empire, they began building homes and buying cattle. Herbert wrote, "I am the cook and my partner tried to make some bread one day and failed so it falls upon me to cook. I am getting rather swell at making bread now and biscuits with a few currants on Sundays as a treat, as they are too expensive for us to indulge in often."

Herbert also created an English favorite for the ranchmen, "I seem to think no one can make bread like me and my success at Yorkshire pudding has been acknowledged by all who have partaken of it as well as pastry. You seem to think it is fun cooking, but I can tell you I don't like it; it is pretty hard work to cook for a lot of hungry men."

Herbert eventually went back to England to marry Margaret Newhall. When they returned to his ranch he and Margaret hired a Chinese cook named Ah. Margaret wrote letters to her mother and some of them included references to the food that was eaten on the ranch in the early 1880s. In August of 1884 she wrote, "We had a splendid shower yesterday and another one today. The ranch looks so beautiful I wish you could see it. We had mushrooms for supper." She also noted her neighbor brought her a basket of peaches. She penned another letter to her mother on July 2, 1885, "The boys, Ned and Phil, are to dine with us and we will have broiled chicken . . . Mike Fagan came out from Tucson yesterday and brought me a little basket of peaches and apricots which are very nice."

CUSTARD PUDDING

SERVES 4–6

  3 egg yolks
  6 tablespoons sugar
  2 cups milk
  1 teaspoon vanilla

Beat the eggs and sugar in a medium bowl and set aside.

Heat the milk over low heat in a medium saucepan until the edges begin to bubble.

Add the vanilla and then gradually add the eggs to the milk, stirring constantly.

Cook over low heat until mixture coats the back of a wooden spoon.

Pour into pudding cups and chill.

RECIPE ADAPTED FROM THE *KANSAS HOME COOK BOOK*, 1874.

SCONES

MAKES ABOUT 8

  2 cups flour
  1 tablespoon baking powder
  ½ teaspoon salt
  ¼ cup sugar
  ½ cup butter
  3 tablespoons light cream or milk
  1 egg, beaten
  ½ cup currants or raisins, optional

Sift the dry ingredients together in a large bowl.

Cut the butter into the ingredients until pea-sized crumbles appear.

Add the light cream and egg and stir until a dough is formed.

Add the currants and knead into the dough.

Roll on a floured surface to an inch thick. Cut into eight diamond shapes or triangles. Place on greased cookie sheet.

Bake for 12–15 minutes in a 425°F oven.

RECIPE ADAPTED FROM THE *IDAHO REGISTER*, DECEMBER 29, 1899.

YORKSHIRE PUDDING

SERVES 6–10

  3 large eggs
  1 cup all-purpose flour
  ¾ cup whole milk
  ½ teaspoon salt
  Vegetable oil or beef drippings

Combine eggs and flour in a large mixing bowl and beat for 5 minutes.

Gradually add the milk and salt and beat until combined.

Allow the batter to rest for an hour.

Preheat oven to 425°F.

Place 1 tablespoon oil into the desired number of cups in a muffin/cupcake pan, and put in the oven for about 10 minutes.

Remove pan from oven and add 3–4 tablespoons batter to each cup.

Bake for 15–20 minutes or until golden.

Remove servings from the pan and set them on paper towels for a minute or 2.

Serve hot.

RECIPE ADAPTED FROM MONTANA'S *BUTTE WEEKLY MINER*, FEBRUARY 4, 1897.

STEWED MUSHROOMS

SERVES 4–6

> 1 pound mushrooms
> 1 cup water
> 1 tablespoon butter
> Juice of a lemon
> ½ teaspoon salt
> ¼ teaspoon fresh ground pepper
> ½ cup light cream
> 1 tablespoon flour

Place the mushrooms, water, butter, lemon, salt, and pepper in a saucepan.

Bring to a boil and cook for 10 minutes, stirring frequently.

In a small bowl combine the cream and flour, and stir to dissolve the flour.

Add the cream and flour to the mushrooms and bring back to a boil.

Serve immediately.

RECIPE ADAPTED FROM THE *KANSAS HOME COOK BOOK*, 1874.

The Boss's House

Mabel and her husband James Madison owned a ranch outside of Alamogordo, New Mexico. She recalled her days on the ranch: "I liked ranch life right from the start, for I rode the range with Jim, learned to cook and eat chuck-wagon food and to ride and rope with the best of them. Our cowpunchers were a jolly bunch and always ready for a good time. We got lots of fun out of rodeos, chuck suppers, roping contests and dances. Our ranch was the J-M ranch, and our cattle was branded with the J on the shoulder, the bar on the side, and the M on the hip. Our ranch cook was famous for his sour dough biscuits. The cowboys called them 'dough gods.'

"And I just wish you could have seen the boys decked out for a round-up; they were as eager to get started as a bunch of school kids. To see them on their prancing ponies with their faces wreathed in smiles was something worthwhile. The cowboys always took the lead. Then came the noisy old mess-wagon with the cook perched on the driver's seat as proud as a peacock because he had a chance to show off his skill in managing a four-hand team of dancing ponies. And last came the horse-wrangler with the reserve horses, called the 'saddle bunch.' Each ranch had its own mess and bed-wagon, and its own set of men. The cattle companies from miles around met at a given point and pitched camp. At mess they usually had bacon, beans, black coffee and warm bread, or as it was called, 'hunk'. After they'd leave I could hear them singing in the distance: 'Oh, I want to be a cowboy and with the cowboys stand, Big spurs upon my boot-heels, A lasso in my hand.' They had good voices too and just seemed to put their hearts and souls into music."

She also recalled the barbecues: "A Calico dress was considered to be good enough for any occasion. When we had a barbecue the men cooked the meat. Sometimes they'd be up all night, turning, basting and keeping the beef from burning. The women baked all the good things they knew how to bake and took them to the barbecue. They usually arrived driving a team of horses and some kind of a wagon, wearing their sunbonnets and old calicos. Of course they brought the children along; it was a regular picnic for them. The cowboys always brought a fiddle and a guitar along and ended up with a shindig. We mostly waltzed, two-stepped or square danced."

Clarice and Jarvis Richards were unlikely ranchers, but Jarvis packed up his Ohio-native wife and headed to Colorado. They ran a cattle ranch with about twenty cowboys, Tex the cook, and Mr. and Mrs. Bohm, who had lived on the ranch for years.

Even though Clarice was settling into ranch life, she had many things to get used to, including the cowboy's way. In her book, *A Tenderfoot Bride*, in which she and her husband were called Mr. and Mrs. Owen Brook, she wrote, "The cook eloped with the best rider on the place, more thrilling and upsetting to my peace of mind than the cloudburst and flood that followed soon after. Twenty-two husky and hungry men wanted three square meals a day, and one inexperienced bride stood between them and starvation. The situation was mutually serious.

"In my need came help. Tex, our coachman on that first drive, saved the day. Shortly after the elopement he came in for supplies for the cowcamp. I was almost hidden by pans of potatoes, and was paring away endlessly. He was very quiet when I explained, but after supper he gathered up the dishes to wash them for me, looking very

Cowboys sitting in the the dirt having their supper, ca. 1907. *Courtesy Library of Congress*

serious. When he had finished, he suddenly turned to me:

"'Say, Mrs. Brook, I've just been studyin'. Jack Brent kin cook for the boys out at camp all right, and if you kin stand it, I kin come in and cook for you. It sure got my goat to see you rastlin' with them potatoes and wearin' yourself out cookin' for these here men.' Good old Tex! That was little short of saintly. Camp cooking where he was autocrat was far more to his taste. He hated 'messin' 'round where there was women,' as he expressed it. Here was sacrifice indeed! Tex scrubbed his hands until they fairly bled, enveloped himself in a large checked gingham apron, and proceeded to act as chef until the eloper had been replaced."

BARBECUED BEEF

SERVES 6–8

> 3 pounds beef, 2-inch thick, like London Broil
> Barbecue dressing (See recipe this page.)

If using coals, get them white and hot. If using a gas grill, turn to high.

Baste the meat with the dressing and then place on the grill.

Sear uncovered for 2–4 minutes on one side for medium rare. Do not press or move the meat.

After desired cooking time is reached, flip the steak, baste with dressing, and grill for 2–4 minutes uncovered.

Baste again, move to a cooler part of the grill, and cover.

Turn and baste occasionally for about 30 minutes.

Allow to rest 5–10 minutes before slicing so the juices will be retained.

BARBECUE DRESSING

MAKES ABOUT 3 CUPS

> 2 cups cider vinegar
> 2 cups canned tomatoes, chopped
> 2 teaspoons red pepper flakes
> 1 teaspoon black pepper
> 1 teaspoon salt
> 2 tablespoons butter

Simmer all the ingredients together until blended. Can be stored in the refrigerator for up to 1 week.

RECIPES ADAPTED FROM *CAMPING AND CAMP COOKING*, 1909.

Wagner Ranch

This ranch is now the Jenner Family Ranch, and the Jenners are the fifth generation of Wagners to work it. According to Gail Jenner, "Our ranch is in the heart of Siskiyou County and a portion of our current ranch has its roots in the Wagner Ranch. It was purchased by Ignace and Mary Ann (Lichtenthaler) Wagner, both of Alsace, France, on March 17, 1874. The original farmhouse on the property was built in 1859, on the hill, but the Wagners built a new home on the flat, opposite the old structure. The original homestead was then used as a 'garage' and the last vestige of it was finally torn down around 2007.

"The first Jenner to arrive in Scott Valley was E. P., who emigrated from Sussex County, England, in 1849. He founded the Union Flour Mill around

A buggy on the Wagner Ranch, Etna, California, in the 1800s. *Courtesy Gail Jenner*

1864 just outside the town of Rough and Ready, now called Etna. With gold miners needing food and supplies, it was E. P.'s nephew, Frank S. Jenner, who followed his uncle to the valley and established a ranch on land straddling the 'Island' in the 1870s, where rich bottomland produces good feed for cattle."

Frank married a woman named Mary "Muzzy" Wagner who cooked on an old woodstove for at least twenty hired hands every day on the ranch her entire married life. Gail recalled, "When my parents were married in 1922, they lived at the ranch, with no electricity or indoor plumbing, with Muzzy and Grandpa Jenner. My mother mentioned she couldn't ask for a nicer mother-in-law than Muzzy as she never created any troubles, and if anything, was always helpful. Brother Jack and I often had lunch with our grandparents and at all times looked forward to a piece of Muzzy's devil's food cake. Muzzy was a fast walker and would go up town to do her shopping. She was never known to drive. She always had a big garden, lots of berries, and [was] most of all famous for her dandelion wine or from other natural resources."

According to Gail there was no "boss's house" and the hired men slept in the bunkhouse, but took their meals in the house. She said, "This was not like what you see in the movies and the hired help ate with the family. These people were not part of any 'elite' class. They were all in it together and were pretty average people and everyone worked. They did have a Chinese cook's helper and launderer who had his own room above the washhouse and he was part of the family for years. It was common in the valley here for the senior Chinese who came to mine but never went home to cook and work at local ranches."

Gail shared Grandma Muzzy's recipe for devil's food cake, which was known to be unbelievably rich and good. According to Gail, Muzzy used her own fresh eggs (she raised over one hundred chickens and turkeys), her own fresh milk, and her own fresh butter. And the flour would have come from the nearby flour mill, which was adjacent to the Wagner Ranch.

MUZZY'S DEVIL'S FOOD CAKE

MAKES 1 CAKE

  1 cup sugar
  1 cup dark chocolate chips
  1 cup milk
  ½ cup butter
  ½ cup brown sugar
  3 egg yolks, beaten
  2 cups flour
  ½ teaspoon baking soda

Melt the sugar, chocolate, and milk together over low heat. Cool slightly.

Cream butter and brown sugar, and add beaten yolks.

Combine flour and baking soda in a separate bowl.

Add dry ingredients alternately with the melted mixture to the creamed mixture, blending well after each addition.

Pour into cake pans that have been greased and floured and bake at 350°F until cake springs back to the touch, 20–25 minutes.

Cool in pans for 10 minutes and then turn onto cake racks to cool completely before frosting.

Frost with Chocolate Frosting, page 76, or a favorite frosting.

Grandma Muzzy made this cake for her family and ranch hands on the Wagner Ranch.

CHOCOLATE FROSTING

FROSTS 1 CAKE

- 5 ounces dark chocolate
- 2 eggs, beaten
- 1 teaspoon cornstarch or flour
- 1 cup milk
- ¼–½ cup sugar, to taste

Place ingredients in a saucepan over low heat.

Stir constantly until all blended and smooth. This will take about 10 minutes and will look like pudding.

Cook until slightly thickened.

Frost cake immediately.

CAKE RECIPE COURTESY OF GAIL JENNER AND SLIGHTLY MODIFIED. FROSTING RECIPE ADAPTED FROM THE *CALIFORNIA RECIPE BOOK*, 1872.

The Mallet Ranch

According to western author Steve Turner, the Mallet was a huge ranch put together by David DeVitt from separate holdings in 1885. It encompassed two hundred square miles in Hockley, Terry, Cochran, and Yoakum Counties. During the winter months the ranch employed only about six men. These six, along with the foreman, the windmill man, and Turner's ancestors, manned the five-room ranch house. The headquarters also had several bunkhouses, sheds, barns, and corrals. Steve's grandfather, Aaron Lloyd Turner, worked as a chuck wagon cook while his grandmother Effie cooked at the ranch house. Aaron was known for his Son of a B Stew and sourdough biscuits.

Steve recalled a family story about his grandmother Effie cooking for the cowboys in the early 1900s: "Grandmother set the plates around one night and one of the hands complained the beans were too salty. She didn't say a word. The next day, he bit into his food and made a terrible face. Grandmother spouted off, 'What's the matter? Your food too salty?!' She had dosed him real good with plenty of salt."

Food on the ranch itself was pretty well varied, but there was no such thing as three squares a day. According to Steve, there were "two squares a day: a big breakfast of eggs, biscuits, bacon, and coffee. Lunch didn't exist west of the Brazos and neither did Sundays. You can rest when you're dead. They would take a couple of cold biscuits and some cooked bacon wrapped up in a bandana for mid-day snacking."

Suppers at the ranch consisted of fried beef, pinto beans, mashed potatoes, and corn bread. During the summer fresh vegetables from the big ranch garden included squash, sweet corn, cucumbers, tomatoes, greens, and black-eyed peas. Steve's grandmother loved to make cakes, and was known for her tall, multilayer chocolate cake for special occasions. Cobblers were the standard dessert for everyday fare. According to Steve, "pies didn't share easily between that many people, but grandmother was noted for her coconut cream pies. This was later."

Canned tomatoes were very popular on ranches and added flavor and variety to plain meats. Dried beans, black-eyed peas, cornmeal, flour, sugar (used sparingly, as it was expensive), salt, and coffee were pantry staples. They also had plenty of beef. Steve also shared that "pork didn't keep worth a darn and they often didn't raise hogs. Bacon and salt pork was readily available and cheap. They did keep chickens for the fresh eggs and the occasional meal of fried chicken. The chickens had to be watched as rattlesnakes and hawks worked peck on them and several kinds of snakes would eat the eggs whole. They pretty well fed themselves from horse droppings in the corral."

COCONUT CREAM PIE

MAKES 1 PIE

- 1 single piecrust
- 2 cups half-and-half
- 3 eggs
- ½ cup sugar
- ¼ cup cornstarch
- 1 tablespoon butter or coconut oil
- ½ cup sweetened, flaked coconut
- 1 teaspoon vanilla extract
- Whipped cream topping
- Toasted coconut for top

Bake piecrust at 350°F for 15 minutes. Set aside.

Whisk together half-and-half and eggs in a small bowl.

Combine sugar and cornstarch in a heavy saucepan and then gradually stir the egg mixture into the sugar mixture.

Bring to a boil over medium heat, stirring constantly. Boil 1 minute.

Remove from heat and stir in butter, coconut and vanilla. Cover with a lid and let stand for 30 minutes. Pour into baked piecrust and cover with whipped cream and toasted coconut. Chill for 4 hours or longer.

WHIPPED CREAM TOPPING

COVERS 1 PIE

- 2 cups whipping cream
- ⅓ cup sugar

Beat whipping cream in a large bowl at high speed with an electric mixer.

Add the sugar and beat until soft peaks form.

Spread over pie filling.

RECIPES ADAPTED FROM THE *FREDERICKSBURG* (TEXAS) *HOME KITCHEN COOK BOOK*, 1916.

These squash cakes were a great way to use an overabundance of squash and get your vegetables too!

FRIED SQUASH CAKES

MAKES ABOUT 8 PANCAKES

  2 cups squash, like zucchini or yellow
  1 cup milk
  1 egg
  ½ teaspoon salt
  ½ teaspoon baking soda
  1 cup flour

To cook squash

Peel and cut the squash into chunks.

Place in a saucepan and add enough water to cover. Boil over high heat until tender. Drain and run the squash through a ricer or mash well.

Strain off any liquid.

To make the cakes

In a large bowl combine the milk and egg and beat well.

Add the salt, baking soda, flour, and 1 cup cooked squash. Mix well and fry as you would for pancakes.

RECIPE ADAPTED FROM THE *DAILY ARKANSAS GAZETTE*, MAY 7, 1882.

BAKED CORN

SERVES 4–6

  2 cups canned corn
  2 eggs, beaten
  1 teaspoon salt
  ¼ teaspoon freshly ground pepper
  1 teaspoon sugar
  2 tablespoons melted butter
  2 cups warm milk

Mix all the ingredients together in a large bowl.

Pour into a buttered baking dish and bake until firm, about 40 minutes, at 350°F.

RECIPES ADAPTED FROM THE *FREDERICKSBURG* (TEXAS) *HOME KITCHEN COOK BOOK*, 1916.

COOKED CUCUMBERS

SERVES 4

- 4 large cucumbers
- ½ cup water
- ¾ cup cider vinegar
- ½ cup sugar

Remove the seeds from the cucumbers and dice into bite-size pieces.

Place all ingredients into a large saucepan and bring to a boil.

Cook for about 25 minutes.

Chill and serve cold.

RECIPES ADAPTED FROM THE *FREDERICKSBURG* (TEXAS) *HOME KITCHEN COOK BOOK*, 1916.

BAKED TOMATOES

SERVES 4–6

- 6 large, firm tomatoes
- 1 tablespoon butter
- 1 small onion, diced
- ¼ cup bread crumbs
- ¼ cup water
- ½ teaspoon salt
- ¼ teaspoon freshly ground pepper

Remove the tops from the tomatoes and scoop out most of the inside. Be sure to leave enough so the tomatoes hold their shape.

Melt the butter in a frying pan over medium heat and then add the onion.

Sauté for about 3 minutes, or until soft but not brown.

Remove from heat and place in a bowl. Add the bread crumbs, water, salt, and pepper, and stir to moisten. Adjust water and seasoning if needed.

Stuff into tomatoes and bake at 375°F for about 15 minutes.

RECIPES ADAPTED FROM THE *FREDERICKSBURG* (TEXAS) *HOME KITCHEN COOK BOOK*, 1916.

GREEN BEANS, HOLLAND STYLE

SERVES 4–6

    1 pound fresh green beans
    2 slices bacon, diced
    1 cup hot water
    ½ teaspoon salt
    ½ teaspoon freshly ground pepper
    1 teaspoon sugar
    1 teaspoon flour
    ¼ cup cider vinegar
    1 tablespoon butter

Snap the ends off the green beans and set aside.

Fry the bacon in a medium saucepan over medium-high heat until crisp.

Add the green beans and then the water and cook over medium heat for about 30 minutes.

Add the salt, pepper, and sugar, and simmer for about 5 minutes or until beans are tender.

Mix the flour with the vinegar and add to the beans.

Add the butter and cook an additional 10 minutes.

RECIPE ADAPTED FROM THE *KANSAS SEMI-WEEKLY CAPITAL*, JULY 17, 1896.

SHIRRED EGGS, TEXAS STYLE

SERVES 4

    Butter for greasing cups
    8 eggs
    ¾ cup cream
    Salt and pepper to taste

Butter ovenproof single-serving bowls or crocks.

Gently break 2 eggs into each baking dish, being careful not to break the yolks.

Add 1 tablespoon of cream per bowl and salt and pepper to taste. Do not stir.

Bake in preheated, 325°F oven for 12–14 minutes. Check the eggs after about 10 minutes baking time to see if the whites are completely set and the yolks are still liquid.

The eggs will continue to cook after being removed from the oven. Serve immediately with toast.

RECIPE ADAPTED FROM THE FORT WORTH, TEXAS, *GAZETTE*, MAY 10, 1891.

PAN-FRIED CHICKEN WITH CREAM GRAVY

SERVES 4–6

½ cup butter or lard
1½ cup flour
Salt and pepper
1 (3-pound) chicken, cut up

Place the butter and/or lard in a large frying pan or dutch oven (cast iron is best) and heat over medium-high heat.

Place the flour, salt, and pepper in shallow bowl.

Rinse the chicken pieces and pat dry.

Coat each piece of chicken with the flour and gently place the chicken in the butter. The butter should sizzle immediately after adding the chicken. Work in small batches to avoid overcrowding. (You can place drained, cooked chicken in a 180°F oven to keep warm while the other pieces are being cooked.)

Fry the chicken until golden brown, turning once, 10–20 minutes, depending on the size of the pieces.

Check for doneness by piercing the meat; the juices should run clear.

When done, place the chicken on paper towels or a wire rack.

CREAM GRAVY

MAKES 1½ CUPS

1 tablespoon butter
1 tablespoon flour
1½ cups milk
Salt and freshly ground pepper to taste

Melt butter in a small saucepan over medium heat and add flour.

Cook for 1 minute and add milk and seasonings.

Stir until thick and pour over chicken.

RECIPES ADAPTED FROM THE *DALLAS MORNING NEWS*, MAY 9, 1886.

SON OF A B STEW, TRADITIONAL

Steve Turner shared his grandfather's recipe for this stew: "Butcher a young still nursing calf. Debone meat, cube, brown in beef fat long bones simmered in cast iron pot to remove all the bone marrow, discard bones add sliced beef heart, browned cubed beef kidneys, marrow gut (part of the stomach that contained curdled milk) sliced thin. Sweetbreads (liver was held out to cook separately as it was too strong flavored), canned tomatoes, onions, salt, pepper, lots of Louisiana hot sauce. Serve with fresh corn bread and cold beer if you have it."

SON OF A B STEW, MODERN

As the traditional recipe has few measurements, as was the custom in the nineteenth century, I've created this modern version based on the directions in the traditional one.

SERVES 6–8

    1 pound beef bones
    1 pound stew beef, cubed
    ½ pound kidneys, cubed
    3 tablespoons beef fat
    1 beef heart
    ½ pound sweetbreads
    1 cup marrow gut (skip if you can't find locally)
    ½ pound liver, cubed
    3–4 medium onions, sliced
    3 cups canned tomatoes
    1–2 teaspoon salt and pepper (to taste)
    Louisiana hot sauce (to taste)
    Water

Place the beef bones in a large stock pot and cover with water.

Simmer on low heat until the marrow is gone from the bones; discard bones. Set pot aside.

Sauté beef and kidneys in beef fat over medium-high heat in a large dutch oven until browned.

Add the remaining ingredients and cover with water. Bring to a boil.

Reduce the heat and simmer until tender, 2–3 hours.

RECIPE CREATED BY THE AUTHOR FROM THE ORIGINAL VERSION.

Chapter Four

COW TOWNS AND STOCKYARD CITIES

The Grub-Pile Call

There's lots o' songs the puncher sang in roundin' up his herds;
The music wasn't very grand, an' neither was the words.
No op'ry air he chanted, when at night he circled 'round
A bunch of restless longhorns that was throwed on their bed-ground;
But any song the cowboy on his lonely beat would bawl,
Wa'n't half as sweet as when the cook would start the grub-pile call.
I've heard 'em warble "Ol' Sam Bass" for hours at a time;
I've listened to the "Dogie Song," that well-known puncher rhyme;
"The Dyin' Cowboy" made me sad, an' "Mustang Gray" brung tears,
While "Little Joe the Wrangler" yet is ringin' in my ears.
But of the songs the puncher sang, I loved the best of all,
That grand ol' chorus when the cook would start the grub-pile call.
There wasn't any sound so sweet in all the wide range land;
There wa'n't a song the puncher was so quick to understand.
No music that he ever heard so filled him with delight
As when he saw the ol' chuck-wagon top a-gleamin' white;
An' like a benediction on his tired ears would fall
The sweetest music ever heard—the welcome grub-pile call.
I've laid at night an' listened to the lowin' of the steers;
I've heard the coyote's melancholy wail ring in my ears.
The croonin' of the night-wind as it swept across the range
Was mournful-like an' dreary, an' it sounded grim an' strange.
But when the break o' day was near, an' from our tarps we'd crawl,
The mornin' song that charmed us was that welcome grub-pile call.

—E. A. Brininstool, *Trail Dust of a Maverick*, 1914

A cow town or stockyard city was a place where the trail ended and the drive was completed. The most well-known were in Kansas because of the Chisholm Trail. However, other places like Colorado, Wyoming, Missouri, New Mexico, Wyoming, Montana, and Nebraska had them as well, because cattle and ranches stretched across the western frontier.

Being a cow town was both a blessing and a curse. It was at the peak of the cattle boom when these cities received the cattle. They benefited from the revenue they earned when the cattle drive ended at their railroad station and the cowboys celebrated. Kansas was filled with cattle towns because many of its cities offered railheads that transported the cattle to Chicago.

While the townsfolk were happy to take the cowboys' and the ranch owners' money from their cattle trade, they did not like their town being turned upside down. Some complained that the cowboys were crude and disrupted their daily lives, and the cattle trampled their crops.

Once the cowboys reached town and corralled the cattle, they were paid for their work. It was natural that they were ready to spend their hard-earned income; they would get a bath and clean duds, and then they would hit the saloons. They whooped it up, ate, drank, and gambled. Many of them also visited the dance halls—which offered more than just dancing—for female companionship.

The trail-weary cowboys often got a bit too rowdy in town. They would drunkenly holler at the moon or shoot up the pretty glasses on a saloon's back bar. It's no wonder so many cow towns had bad reputations and were often "abused" by the cowboys. Despite what you see in the movies, most cowboys had honor. If they did shoot up a saloon after a wild night, they usually went back to the saloon the next day. They apologized to the owner and offered to pay for the damages. Once they had either spent most of their pay or done enough celebrating, they headed back down the trail for their respective ranches.

Another type of cow town was a town surrounded by cattle ranches. These were found throughout the West, including Texas, Arizona, Colorado, California, New Mexico, Wyoming, Montana, Oregon, the Dakotas, and a few others. The cowboys and cattlemen and their families would occasionally go into town for a meal at a restaurant or hotel. In this section, you'll find the typical meals served at both types of cow towns.

Kansas Cow Towns

From the 1860s to the 1880s, Abilene, Caldwell, Dodge City, Newton, Trail City, and Wichita saw many a cowboy and thousands of cattle barrel into town in late summer. When the cowboys reached these cow towns, a mighty celebration took place. They wanted women, clean clothes, hot baths, stiff drinks, and delicious meals that didn't consist of beans.

Since these towns were doing well with cattle money and other business, restaurants and hotels served almost anything.

The Douglas Avenue House in Wichita offered this menu in 1872:

Soup: Mock Turtle

Boiled: Ham, Corned Beef, Tongue

Roast: Rib of Beef, Sirloin Beef, Rib of Veal, and Pork

Relishes: Worcestershire Sauce, Cheese, French Mustard, Cucumbers, Tomato Catsup, Cucumber Pickles, Chow Chow, Radishes, and Cold Slaw

Entrees: Chicken Pie, Baked Ham Spiced with Champagne Sauce, Tripe a La Creole, Beef a La Mode, Calf's Liver Brazed with Onions

Vegetables: Mashed Potatoes, Boiled Potatoes, Green (Fresh) Corn, Stewed Squash, Cabbage, and Stewed Tomatoes

Pastry and Pudding: Strawberry Pie, Peach Pie, Steam Suet Pudding with Wine Sauce, and Lemon Pie

Dessert: Fruit Cake, Marble Cake, Muskmelon, Pecans, Ice Cream, Soda Cake, Yankee Doughnuts, Watermelon, Gold Cake, Almonds and Raisins, and Silver Cake

Served with: Coffee or English Breakfast Tea

CHICKEN PIE

SERVES 4–6

> 4 pounds chicken, boneless breasts and legs
> 2 cups water
> 1 onion, diced
> 1 teaspoon sage
> 1 teaspoon salt
> Freshly ground pepper to taste
> 4–6 potatoes, peeled and cubed
> Biscuit topping (See recipe on facing page.)

Place the chicken, water, onion, sage, salt, and pepper in a large stockpot.

Bring to a boil, cook for 15 minutes, and then add the potatoes.

Cook another 15 minutes or until chicken is done.

Remove from the pot and reserve the broth. Skim any foam from the top.

Place in a baking dish and top with biscuit topping.

Bake at 350°F for about 20 minutes or until the biscuit is golden. The broth should soak into the biscuit topping.

BISCUIT TOPPING

MAKES ENOUGH FOR 1 CHICKEN PIE

2 cups flour
1 teaspoon baking powder
½ teaspoon salt
¾ cup milk

Combine dry ingredients in a bowl.

Slowly add the milk to make moist enough to spoon over the chicken.

RECIPES ADAPTED FROM THE *KANSAS HOME COOK BOOK*, 1874.

BEEF A LA MODE

SERVES 6–8

1 (4-pound) round roast
8 pieces salt pork or bacon
¼ teaspoon salt
¼ teaspoon freshly ground pepper
½ cup flour
¼ cup butter or margarine
⅓ cup diced celery
1 sprig parsley
⅓ cup diced turnip
1 bay leaf
⅓ cup diced carrots
1 cup cooking Sherry
⅓ cup diced onion

Using a knife, make 8 slits horizontally in the meat. Push the pieces of salt pork or bacon into the slits. Season the meat with the salt and pepper, and then dredge through the flour.

In a large dutch oven, melt the butter or margarine over medium heat.

Add the roast and brown on all sides.

Add the remaining ingredients to the pan; be sure to put everything around the roast, not on it. Add enough water to cover the roast halfway.

Cover and cook over low heat for 4 hours. Do not allow the water to boil.

When the roast is tender, remove and place it on a serving platter.

Strain the liquid and set it aside for the gravy.

BEEF GRAVY

4 tablespoons butter or margarine
4 tablespoons flour
Reserved liquid from roast
Salt and pepper to taste

In the pan in which the roast was cooked, melt butter or margarine, stir in the flour, and cook for 3–4 minutes, or until golden.

Gradually add the reserved liquid and whisk for 5 minutes or until thick.

Season with salt and pepper to taste.

Pour the gravy over the roast or serve on the side.

RECIPES ADAPTED FROM THE *KANSAS CITY TIMES*, JUNE 19, 1887.

BOILED POTATOES

½ teaspoon salt
6–8 large red or gold potatoes (not russet),
    peeled and cut into chunks
¼ cup butter
½ teaspoon salt
¼ teaspoon freshly ground pepper
Fresh chopped parsley

Add salt to a large stockpot of water and bring to a boil over high heat.

Add potatoes and cook for 10–15 minutes or until tender.

Remove and drain. Also remove any excess water from the pot.

Return potatoes to the pot and turn the heat to low. Add the butter, salt, and pepper. Heat and stir gently, long enough to coat the potatoes.

Garnish with fresh chopped parsley.

RECIPE ADAPTED FROM THE *IDAHO DAILY STATESMAN*, MAY 25, 1897.

LEMON PIE

MAKES 1 PIE

1½ cups sugar
⅓ cup cornstarch
1½ cups water
3 egg yolks, beaten
3 tablespoons butter
2 teaspoons grated lemon peel
½ cup lemon juice
1 baked (9-inch) piecrust

Mix sugar and cornstarch in a medium saucepan and then gradually whisk in the water.

Cook over medium heat, stirring constantly, until mixture thickens and boils. Boil and stir for 1 minute.

Place the egg yolks in a small bowl. Slowly pour half of the hot sugar mixture into the egg yolks, whisking constantly so the eggs don't scramble.

Once tempered (or warmed up), stir them back into hot mixture in saucepan. Boil and stir constantly for 2 minutes.

Remove from the heat and add butter, lemon peel, and lemon juice, and stir to combine.

Pour into the baked piecrust.

Spread meringue (see recipe this page) around the edges and work toward center. Leave a space in the center or add a dollop of egg whites.

Bake at 400°F for 10–20 minutes or until meringue is golden.

Cool for 30 minutes and then refrigerate a minimum of 4 hours before serving.

MERINGUE

MAKES ENOUGH FOR 1 PIE

> 2 egg whites
> 2 tablespoons sugar

By hand or with an electric mixer, beat egg whites and sugar in a bowl at high speed until stiff peaks form.

RECIPES ADAPTED FROM *KANSAS HOME COOK BOOK*, 1874.

Lemon pie was a favorite during the nineteenth century.

In April 1874 cowboys may have strolled into Wichita's three-story Occidental Hotel and enjoyed this menu:

Soup: Mock Turtle

Boiled and Roasts: Whitefish with Egg Sauce, Ham, Corned Beef, Beef Tongue, Leg of Mutton, Loin of Veal, Stuffed Chicken with Dressing, Cold Ham, and Corned Beef Tongue

Entrees: Calf's Brains, Breaded Round of Veal, Larded And Potted Duck With Green (Fresh) Turnips, Boar's Head With Savory Jelly, Fillets of Mutton With Fine Herb Sauce, Calves' Feet, German-Style, Ames' Sugar-Cured Hams and Champagne Sauce, Boned Turkey With Cranberry Sauce, and Pilots of Turkey, Turkish-Style

Relishes: Worcestershire Sauce, Halford Sauce, French Mustard, Cheese, Walnuts, Cut Up, Tomato Catsup, Cucumber Pickles, and Cold Slaw

Pastry and Pudding: Lemon Pie, Currant Pudding with Brandy Sauce, Cranberry Pie, Boston Cream Cakes, Blackberry Pie, and Blanch Mange

Dessert: Currant Cake, French Cake, Jelly Cake, Silver Cake, Raisins, Apples, Almonds, and Banana Ice Cream

Served with: Coffee, Tea, or Roman Punch

CORNED BEEF

SERVES 4–6

4 pounds corned beef
4 cups water
6 potatoes, cut up
6 carrots, peeled and cut up
1 turnip, cubed
2 large onions, chopped
1 bay leaf
½ teaspoon freshly ground pepper

Put the beef in a large dutch oven; add the water and bring to a boil.

Cover and simmer over low heat for about 2 hours.

Add the potatoes, carrots, turnip, onions, bay leaf, and pepper.

Cook for another hour. The meat and vegetables will be tender when done.

RECIPE ADAPTED FROM *SCAMMELL'S CYCLOPEDIA OF VALUABLE RECEIPTS*, 1897.

HAM WITH CHAMPAGNE VINEGAR SAUCE

This recipe is a good way to serve leftover ham. If you are already using leftovers, skip to the champagne sauce.

SERVES 4–6

1 (5–7) pound ham
Whole cloves, about 30 depending on ham size
½ cup brown sugar
½ cup chicken stock or white cooking wine
Champagne Vinegar Sauce (See recipe this page.)

Cut slits in the ham ¼-inch deep and 1 inch apart.

Place the ham in a baking pan, fat side up. Push the cloves into the slits.

Mix the brown sugar and stock in a small bowl and spread over the ham, reserving some of the mixture.

Bake at 350°F for 3½ hours, basting occasionally with the sugar mixture.

Check with a meat thermometer to ensure doneness with an internal temperature of 140°F.

Allow the ham to rest for 10 minutes and then slice. Serve with the sauce.

RECIPE ADAPTED FROM THE KANSAS *TOPEKA DAILY STATE JOURNAL*, DECEMBER 15, 1915.

CHAMPAGNE VINEGAR SAUCE

MAKES ENOUGH TO SERVE WITH A 5–7 POUND HAM

¼ cup butter
¼ cup chopped carrot
¼ cup sliced onion
6 peppercorns
1 bay leaf
1 sprig thyme
¼ cup chopped fresh parsley
5 tablespoons flour
2 cups beef stock
½ cup champagne vinegar
1 tablespoon powdered sugar

Melt the butter in a large saucepan over medium heat.

Add the carrot, onion, and seasonings to the pan and sauté until lightly browned.

Add the flour and cook until it starts to brown as well.

Gradually add the stock and cook until slightly thickened.

Strain the sauce and discard the vegetables.

Return the sauce to the heat and cook for 5 minutes.

Add the vinegar and sugar; heat through and serve.

RECIPE ADAPTED FROM *SCAMMELL'S CYCLOPEDIA OF VALUABLE RECEIPTS*, 1897.

SILVER CAKE

MAKES 1 CAKE

3 cups sugar
1 cup butter, softened
3 cups flour
2 teaspoons baking powder
1 cup milk
1 teaspoon lemon or almond extract
6 egg whites

Add sugar, butter, flour, baking powder, milk, and the flavoring into large mixer bowl. Beat on low for about 1 minute.

Scrape down and beat on high speed for 2 minutes, scraping bowl occasionally.

Add the egg whites and beat an additional 2 minutes on high speed.

Pour into 2 cake pans or a tube pan that has been greased and floured. Bake at 350°F for 40–45 minutes or until a wooden pick inserted in center comes out clean.

Allow to rest in pans for 10 minutes and then turn onto cake racks to cool completely.

RECIPE ADAPTED FROM THE *DENVER POST*, APRIL 23, 1896.

New Mexico Cow Towns

According to cattleman and former New Mexico governor, James F. Hinkle, Roswell saw its share of cowboy activity. Roswell was a cow town in the 1880s, and, as Hinkle recalled, "From 1885, until the middle nineties Roswell was the cattle center for all the spring round-ups and spring drives to shipping points. Round-up wagons and cattle and cowboys in their high-heeled boots, leather 'chaps' and ten 'gallon hats,' would come in from the range from as far north as Fort Sumner, and south as Pecos City, Texas a distance of about two hundred and fifty miles. Some of them often had not seen a woman, or a post office, or store for as long as six months or more. Roswell, the 'blow-off-town' with its one adobe store lighted by two kerosene lamps with tin reflectors at the back, which were hung at each end of the store, one near the post office which was run in a corner of the store, and one hotel of the town also constructed of adobe, seemed a 'City of Bright Lights' to the carefree cowboys so long away from civilization.

"The ones who had not disposed of their monthly wage, from twenty-five to thirty dollars, would usually engage a 'room' at the hotel, which would be a bed in the attic which was sleeping quarters for all guests. Cowboys, doctors, lawyers and an occasional Territorial Governor (George Curry) would share the conveniences or inconveniences, with no favorites shown no matter what their social standing might be.

"If there were any church meetings during round up times in Roswell or 'bailien,' it made little difference which to the cowboys, they would

Cowboys enjoying their chuck wagon meal after a hard day's work, ca. 1880–1919. *Courtesy Library of Congress*

be there literally 'with bells on' (jingling spur) which they never removed for church service, or the dance. When the round-up came to town, it was hailed so enthusiastically with shouts of joy from the young people: 'The roundup's Coming!', as I remember shouting, when a child on the Mississippi River when a boat appeared 'The steamboat's Coming!' for the 'chuck' wagon dinners or suppers, if one was fortunate enough to stand in favor with the cowboys, and knew they would receive invitations to them, were looked forward to eagerly by both young and old people of Roswell.

"The round up wagon, 'chuck,' is served at the noon meal, on pioneers day at the end of the trail or parade, during the fall every year in Roswell, and the barbecued beef and mutton, 'son-of-a-gun,' ice cream and coffee, served to the 'old timers' is hard to beat, but somehow it lacks something in the flavor—that cannot be reproduced—of the old chuck-wagon meals of stews, prunes, frijoles and sour-dough biscuit cooked on a camp-fire, by a chuck-wagon cook. Compared with the price in 1868 that John Chisum received, averaging eighteen dollars a head, it seems that the cattle business was not very promising and comparing John Chisum's average price per head with the twenty-five to thirty dollars per head paid at the present time, the cattle industry has improved and far ahead of ahead of what it ever [?] in the Southeastern New Mexico."

STRAWBERRY ICE CREAM

MAKES 4 QUARTS

  2 cups sugar
  1 pint milk
  1 teaspoon cornstarch
  1 egg, beaten well
  1 quart heavy cream
  1 teaspoon vanilla
  2 cups strawberries, pureed

Heat sugar, milk, cornstarch, and egg in a large saucepan over medium-low heat.

Stir to combine, and cook until cornstarch has dissolved; let cool.

Once cooled, add the cream, vanilla, and strawberry puree.

Freeze according to ice cream machine instructions.

RECIPE ADAPTED FROM IOWA'S *SIOUX CITY JOURNAL*, JUNE 18, 1895.

BEEF STEW

SERVES ABOUT 4

  1 pound stew meat, cut into pieces
  3 onions, sliced
  3 carrots, sliced
  6 potatoes, cut into chucks
  1 teaspoon salt
  Pepper to taste

Place all the ingredients in a stew pot and cover with water.

Bring to a boil.

Reduce heat, cover, and simmer for 2 hours or until everything is tender.

RECIPE ADAPTED FROM NEW MEXICO'S *CARRIZOZO NEWS*, NOVEMBER 17, 1911.

SOURDOUGH BISCUITS

The traditional recipe does not call for baking powder, but it can aid the rising and baking time.

MAKES ABOUT 8

  2 cups flour
  1 teaspoon salt
  2 tablespoons sugar
  3 tablespoons baking powder, optional
  2 tablespoons butter
  2 cups fresh starter (See recipe in chapter 1.)
  Flour, for kneading
  Melted butter for dipping

Combine the flour, salt, and sugar together in a large bowl. If using baking powder, add it here.

Cut in the butter until it crumbles into pea-sized pieces.

Add the starter and stir to combine.

Mix dough until blended. The dough should be soft. Pinch off 2-inch balls and dip each ball into the melted butter. Pack snugly in a baking pan and allow to rest for 2 hours.

If using baking powder, bake 10–12 minutes at 350°F. If not using it, then bake at 425°F for about 20 minutes.

RECIPE ADAPTED FROM MISSOURI'S *KANSAS CITY TIMES*, JANUARY 2, 1887.

Las Vegas, New Mexico, saw its share of cattle and had a large number of ranches. Those who wanted a meal out could dine at the Plaza Hotel, which was operated by Mrs. Sampson. Her Sunday bill of fare included:

Soup: Potage de Creole

Fish: Baked Mackinaw Trout, Sauce Hollandaise

Roasts: Roast beef with brown gravy, small ribs of beef with browned potatoes, loin of pork with applesauce, stuffed leg of mutton

Game: Shoulder of Venison with Jelly, Baked Turkey with Cranberry Sauce, Salmi of Domestic Duck Au Champagne, and Fricassee of Spring Chicken Au Royale

Entrees: Spring Lamb Potpie, Baked Yorkshire Pie, Hunter's Style, and Oyster Patties a La Toulouse

Vegetables: Stewed Tomatoes, Cabbage, Parsnips and Cream, String Beans, and Boiled, Mashed, or Browned Potatoes

Pastry: Lemon Pie, Blackberry Pie, Pumpkin Pie, and Lemon Ice Cream with Jelly Cake

Served with: Tea, Iced Tea, French Drip Coffee, and Cheese

SPRING LAMB POTPIE

MAKES 4–6 SERVINGS

1½ pound lamb
½ teaspoon salt
¼ teaspoon freshly ground pepper
2 tablespoons butter
1 onions, diced
⅓ cup flour
1 cup chicken stock
1 pint canned tomatoes, strained
1 tablespoon fresh parsley, chopped
1 piecrust

Cut the lamb into cubes; add salt and pepper, and then set aside.

Melt the butter in a frying pan over medium-high heat.

Add the lamb and cook until browned on all sides.

Remove from the pan and set aside.

Add the onions and cook until tender, about 10 minutes.

Add flour and cook for 1 minute and then add the stock.

Add the tomatoes and cook over medium heat for 5 minutes or until thickened.

Add the lamb, and stir.

Place the lamb filling in a baking dish and top with the parsley. Cover with the piecrust and bake at 400°F for about 25 minutes or until done.

RECIPE ADAPTED FROM THE OMAHA, NEBRASKA, *WORLD-HERALD*, APRIL 30, 1899.

STEWED TOMATOES

SERVES 2–4

    1 (28-ounce) can tomatoes
    ½ teaspoon salt
    ¼ teaspoon freshly ground pepper
    1 tablespoon butter

Place the tomatoes with their liquid in a large saucepan.

Cover and cook over medium-low heat for 30 minutes.

Add the salt, pepper, and butter and cook uncovered for 10 minutes.

RECIPE ADAPTED FROM GRAND FORKS, NORTH DAKOTA'S *DAILY HERALD*, SEPTEMBER 16, 1899.

BLACKBERRY PIE

MAKES 1 PIE

    ½ cup sugar
    3 cups blackberries
    1 tablespoon flour
    2 piecrusts, unbaked
    Milk

Combine sugar, berries, and flour in a mixing bowl, and stir to coat the berries.

Line a pie pan with 1 crust and pour in the berries.

Cover with the second piecrust and brush with milk.

Bake at 350°F for 35–40 minutes or until the crust is golden.

RECIPE ADAPTED FROM THE IOWA *SIOUX CITY JOURNAL*, MAY 28, 1895.

LEMON ICE CREAM

MAKES 1 QUART

    2 cups heavy cream
    1 cup milk
    1½ cups sugar
    ½ cup freshly squeezed lemon juice or 1
        tablespoon lemon extract

Mix all ingredients in a large bowl and stir to combine until sugar is dissolved.

Freeze according to ice cream machine instructions.

RECIPE ADAPTED FROM WICHITA, KANSAS'S *THURSDAY AFTERNOON COOKING CLUB'S COOK BOOK*, 1922.

Socorro County traces its cattle history to the railroad in the 1880s. The railroad not only brought miners and businessmen, but it also brought cattlemen to Socorro County. The town of Magdalena was considered the end of the trail in 1885 for cattle drives. A spur line was built from Socorro to Magdalena to transport the cattle and other goods. From 1885 until 1916, thousands of cattle were brought to town from the West via the historic Stock Driveway into the stockyards.

Mrs. Wintermute was the proprietor of the Depot Lunch Counter and served many a cowboy and cattleman. Here is the menu of her establishment:

Meats: Fried Chicken, Beef Stew, and Roast Mutton

Vegetables: Cream Potatoes, Green (fresh) Corn, and String Beans

Bread: Corn and White

Pickles: Beets and Cucumbers

Dessert: Pudding, Baked Apple Dumplings, Apple and Custard Pie, Banana Ice Cream, Lemonade, and Soda

Mrs. Wintermute noted in her 1897 newspaper ad, "Ice cream ten cents a dish. I serve lunch at all hours during the day, and good meals every day of the week. All my fresh meats come from Albuquerque. All are respectfully invited to call and try my meals, lunches, fruits, candies, cigars, etc."

BAKED APPLE DUMPLINGS

Did you know the term *green* referred to fruit that was fresh and not dried?

MAKES 6

    6 large apples
    ¾ teaspoon cinnamon
    ½ cup sugar
    1 double piecrust, unbaked
    6 teaspoons butter

Core, slice, and peel the apples.

Place in a bowl with the cinnamon and sugar and stir to coat.

Roll the piecrust dough on a floured surface to ⅛-inch thick.

Use a small saucer to cut out circles.

Place a few apple slices and 1 teaspoon butter on half the circle.

Wet the edges of the dough with water and fold in half. Seal with a fork.

Bake on a greased baking sheet at 350°F for 25–30 minutes or until the apples are fork tender.

RECIPE ADAPTED FROM THE *ALBUQUERQUE MORNING DEMOCRAT*, DECEMBER 1, 1895.

CUCUMBER PICKLES

YIELDS ABOUT 7 PINTS

¾ cup sugar
½ cup canning salt
1 quart vinegar
1 quart water
8 pounds pickling cucumbers (4–6 inches long)
1 garlic clove per jar, peeled (or a piece of
    fresh sliced horseradish, which was more
    common than the garlic we use today)
Crushed red pepper flakes (¼ teaspoon per jar)
Mustard seed (¼ teaspoon per jar)
Dill weed, fresh (1–2 sprigs per jar)
Pint jars (about 7)

Combine the sugar, salt, vinegar, and water in a large saucepan and bring to a boil. Simmer for 15 minutes.

Meanwhile, place cucumbers (whole or sliced), a clove of garlic, crushed red pepper flakes, mustard seed, and dill into sterilized jars. It's important to keep the jars hot so they will not crack when adding the hot liquid. Do this by leaving them in the sterilizing pot until ready to use.

Pour hot liquid into the jars, leaving ¼-inch head space.

Clean edges of jar and seal.

Process in boiling water for 15 minutes to begin the pickling process.

RECIPE ADAPTED FROM MISSOURI'S *ST. LOUIS REPUBLIC*, APRIL 2, 1898.

In April 1898 the Silver City, New Mexico, newspaper, *The Eagle*, predicted the demise of the cowboy. According to the article, "The days of the old time cowboy are vanishing and he is fast becoming associated with memories of the 'trail,' the 'chuck-wagon' and the 'round-up.' In fact, all the time-honored features of the business, clothed as they are with that tinge of romance which has always attached itself to the free life of the great plains of the west, are being classed among the things 'that were.' No more selling of a 'brand' nowadays, with the purchaser to hunt up his own stock and do his own counting. A maverick is now unknown quantity in a well regulated range and cattle are sold and bought with the same precision and exercise of business rules as are used by the merchant in disposing of his goods. Cattle are now sold by the herd[. I]t is quite likely that in a few years the cowboy of other days will create as much of a sensation in the southwest as he would in some staid old New England town."

MENU.

Potage:
Creme d' asperges.
Hors d' oeuvres.
Saucisson, beurre, olives, sardines.

Entrees:
Riz de veau aux petits pois.
Filets mignon, sauce madere.

Entremet:
Omlette aurhum.
Roti.
Cailles sur canape.

Desserts:
Fruits, roquefort.
Mince pie, apple pie.
Cafe, fine champagne.
Champagne monopole, potent canet.
Cigars.

Menus during the Victorian West era were often printed in French. Wonder how the cowboy knew what to order? From the *Omaha Daily Bee*, January 21, 1891.

Nebraska Cow Towns

Omaha was a stockyard town from the early 1870s to well into the early 1900s. Like other cow towns with stockyards, it was on the Union Pacific Railroad's route.

In 1891 a new restaurant opened in Omaha and despite many complaints of others using French for their menus, this one was in French, too. However, the name of the establishment was, Restaurant Francais, and its owners were French, so they did have a legitimate reason for using French.

Soup: Cream of Asparagus with Hors d'oeuvres, Sausage, Butter, Olives, and Sardines

Entrees: Veal with Rice and Petite Peas and Filet Mignon with Madeira Sauce

Entremets (between servings): Omelet with Rum, Toasted Bread, Quail on Toast

Desserts: Fruits, Roquefort, Mince Pie, Apple Pie, Coffee, Fine Champagne, Champagne Monopole, Pontent Canet (Bordeaux), and Cigars

ROAST QUAIL ON TOAST

SERVES 4

- 4 quail
- Salt and pepper to taste
- 1 tablespoon butter
- 1 cup water
- 1 tablespoon flour
- 4 pieces toasted bread

Sprinkle the quail with salt and pepper inside and out, and rub some butter over them.

Bake in a 350°F oven for about 45 minutes. When halfway done, pour water into the pan.

When done, drain the broth, reserving the liquid, and allow the birds to rest.

Remove meat from the bone.

In a small pan, cook butter and flour for 1 minute. Add the pan liquid and cook over medium heat until thick.

Place a piece of toast on each plate, divide the meat of each quail and place on toast. Divide the sauce and pour over each quail.

RECIPE ADAPTED FROM *SCAMMELL'S CYCLOPEDIA OF VALUABLE RECEIPTS*, 1897.

SAUSAGE

MAKES 2 POUNDS

- 2 pounds lean pork
- 1 pound pork fat
- 1½ teaspoons salt
- 1 teaspoon black pepper
- ½ teaspoon cayenne
- 1 garlic clove
- 1 bay leaf
- 1 teaspoon sage
- Pinch of mace
- 1 teaspoon allspice

Grind all ingredients together until fine and refrigerate overnight.

Shape into patties and freeze or cook immediately.

RECIPE ADAPTED FROM THE *LUBBOCK AVALANCHE*, OCTOBER 9, 1919.

CREAM OF ASPARAGUS SOUP

SERVES 4

1 pound asparagus
2 tablespoons butter
3 tablespoons flour
4 cups milk
1 cup water
1 stalk celery
1 sprig fresh thyme
4 sprigs fresh parsley
1 bay leaf
1 teaspoon salt
¼ teaspoon freshly ground pepper
Butter and croutons for garnish

Wash the asparagus and cut off the tips.

Either steam or boil the tips until tender, drain, and set aside. Reserve the tips for garnishing.

Melt the butter in a large stockpot over medium heat.

Once the butter is melted, add the flour and cook for 1 minute.

Whisk in the milk and water and stir until thickened.

Reduce the heat to low and add the asparagus stalks and remaining ingredients, and cook for 30 minutes or until asparagus is tender. Do not let the milk come to a boil.

Strain the soup and return to the pot.

Taste for seasoning and add the asparagus tips.

Serve with a dot of butter and croutons.

RECIPE ADAPTED FROM MISSOURI'S *KANSAS CITY STAR*, AUGUST 17, 1894.

Strained cream soups were very popular during the nineteenth century.

Colorado Cow Towns

Cattle were driven to Denver because of the Burlington and Union Pacific Railroads. Denver had stockyards as early as 1865, and cowboys and ranchers alike streamed into the city. In 1881 Denver had the Union Stockyards, where cattle were corralled until they were loaded on the trains. The stockyards changed names and owners over the years, but Denver remained a cattle town—and one of sophistication at that.

Moon's Oyster Ocean restaurant offered diners chicken giblet soup, broiled trout, stuffed roast tame duck, giblet patties, and roast beef and mutton in 1880.

Restaurateur Jack Lambert offered a slightly more upscale menu than Moon's and all for fifty cents:

Roasts: Pork with Cranberry Sauce, Pork, and Corned Beef and Cabbage

Vegetables: Mashed potatoes, Green peas, and Green Corn

Bread: White, Graham, and Corn

Pastry: Pudding, Pie—Two Kinds, Fruits, Tea and Coffee

WHITE BREAD

MAKES 1 LOAF

1 package yeast
1 tablespoon sugar
¼ cup warm water (110°F)
¼ cup buttermilk, scalded (110°F)
¼ cup butter, softened
1 teaspoon salt
2 eggs, lightly beaten
3–3½ cups bread flour
2 teaspoon butter, melted

In a small bowl, combine the yeast and sugar.

Pour the warm water over this mixture and it set aside.

Put the scalded milk, softened butter, and salt in a large mixing bowl.

Add the yeast mixture, eggs, and 1 cup of the flour.

Mix well, and add enough additional flour to form a soft but not sticky dough.

Knead on a floured surface for about 10 minutes. You will know that you have kneaded enough when you press a finger in the dough and it bounces back.

Place the dough in a lightly oiled bowl, turn to coat the surface, and cover with a towel or plastic wrap.

Allow the dough to double in size in a warm place, about 1 hour.

Remove the dough from the bowl and roll into a rectangular shape on a floured surface.

Starting at a shorter end, roll the dough up like a jelly roll. Tuck the ends under and place in a greased 9-inch loaf pan. Allow this to rise under a towel in a warm place until doubled.

Once the dough has risen again, brush the top with the melted butter and bake at 375°F for 30 minutes.

Remove the bread from the pan and cool on a cake rack.

RECIPE ADAPTED FROM THE *COLORADO COOK BOOK*, 1883.

In 1885 Denver's Maison Doree at 401 Curtis Street offered a Sunday dinner from five to eight in the evening. Meals cost seventy-five cents and included half a bottle of wine.

Soup: Consommé and Chicken

Fish: Tenderloin of Sole, sauce Tartar

Entrees: Filet of Beef with Mushrooms, Salmi of Duck and Olives, and Banana Fritters

Roasts: Turkey and Cranberry, Lamb in Mint Sauce, Beef, Pork, Mutton, and Veal, Stuffed

Dessert: Kirsch and Rum Omelet and Chartreuse, Pies, Cakes, Fruits, Nuts, Cheese, and Black Coffee

CONSOMMÉ

MAKES 2½ QUARTS

2 pounds lean round steak
¼ cup shortening
1 pound beef bones or beef ribs
3 quarts water
2 cups chicken stock
3 egg whites, slighty frothed
½ cup diced carrot
½ cup diced turnip
½ cup diced celery
1 small onion, sliced
2 garlic cloves
2 sprigs thyme
1 tablespoon salt
1 teaspoon whole peppercorns
1 sprig marjoram
2 sprigs parsley
1 bay leaf

Cut beef into 1-inch cubes.

Brown half the beef in the shortening in a large stockpot.

Add the remaining meat, bones, and the water. Let stand for ½ hour.

Heat slowly to boiling and simmer for 3 hours; remove scum as it forms.

Add the chicken stock and simmer for 1 additional hour. Add the egg whites, vegetables, and seasonings. Simmer for another hour. Remove any fat from the top, strain the consommé through cheesecloth, and let cool.

RECIPE ADAPTED FROM WICHITA, KANSAS'S *THURSDAY AFTERNOON COOKING CLUB'S COOK BOOK*, 1922.

TENDERLOIN OF SOLE

Did you know that sole and flounder are basically the same? When the Europeans came to the Americas, they called the North American flounder *sole* because it looked like a fish they were familiar with in their countries.

SERVES 2–4

    1 pound flounder fillets
    Salt and pepper to taste
    Butter

Salt and pepper the fillets and place in a shallow baking dish.

Dot with pieces of butter and cover with foil.

Bake at 350°F for about 15 minutes or until fish can be flaked with a fork.

Serve with tartar sauce (see recipe this page) or drizzle pan butter over top.

RECIPE ADAPTED FROM THE *KANSAS HOME COOK BOOK*, 1874.

TARTAR SAUCE

MAKES 1 CUP

    1 cup mayonnaise
    1 tablespoon chopped capers
    1 tablespoon fresh chopped parsley
    1 tablespoon fresh chopped chives or onions
    1 tablespoon chopped green olives
    1 tablespoon chopped sweet pickles
    1 teaspoon yellow mustard
    1 tablespoon vinegar

Combine all the ingredients in a bowl, blend well, and allow to chill.

RECIPE ADAPTED FROM MISSOURI'S *KANSAS CITY STAR*, SEPTEMBER 9, 1900.

BANANA FRITTERS

6 bananas
1 tablespoon lemon juice
2 eggs, beaten
1 tablespoon butter, melted
1 tablespoon sugar
1½ cups flour
1 teaspoon baking powder
Oil for frying
Sugar for finishing

Mash bananas in a large mixing bowl.

Add lemon juice, eggs, and melted butter, and mix well.

In a small bowl, combine sugar, flour, and baking powder.

Add this mixture to the bananas and stir until blended.

Heat 1 inch of oil to 365°F in a large dutch oven.

Once the oil is hot, gently drop batter by tablespoon, working in small batches, and fry until golden on all sides, 2 minutes.

Drain on paper towels.

Roll in granulated sugar.

RECIPE ADAPTED FROM WICHITA, KANSAS'S *THURSDAY AFTERNOON COOKING CLUB'S COOK BOOK*, 1922.

Chapter Five

HOLIDAYS AND CELEBRATIONS, COWBOY-STYLE

Christmas Week in Sagebrush

It is Christmas week in Sagebrush, and the old town's only store
Never had, sence it was opened, such a run o' trade before.
Ev'ry rancher is a-blowin' his "dinero" full and free,
Buyin' gim-cracks for the young'uns to put on the Christmas tree.
The cowboys ride in muffled in their wolf-skin coats and chaps,
And the rancher's wife is wearin' all her extry furs and wraps;
'Cuz nobody takes no chances on a norther breakin' loose,
Fer a blizzard on the prairy's purty apt to raise the deuce.
The ponies that are standin' all a-shiver at the rack,
Champ their bits, and paw and nicker for their riders to come back;
Ev'ry poker joint is runnin', and there's faro and roulette,
And the booze-joints are a-grabbin' all the punchers they can get.
The picter show is crowded full o' riders off the range
Who are watchin' actor cowboys doin' stunts that's new and strange;
Ev'ry film brings groans and hisses, o'cuz the guys upon the screen
Go through lots o' monkey bizness that a cow ranch never seen.
From the dance halls comes the echoes of a squeaky violin,
Where the painted dames are ropin' all the gay cowpunchers in;
For it's Christmas week in Sagebrush, and there won't a puncher go
Back to ride the wintry ranges when he has a cent to blow!

—E. A. Brininstool, *Trail Dust of a Maverick*, 1914

Holidays and celebrations were enjoyed by cowboys and by the ranchers. Those festive events could vary quite a bit depending upon which you were.

Cowboys living on their own may have stood at the bar in a lonely saloon or passed the day alone. Depending upon where they were, some didn't even know a holiday was taking place. Sometimes the men on the trail were invited to share Christmas with local homesteaders.

Now if you were living on a ranch, whether it be as the owner or as a hired hand, things were different. The two largest celebrations on the ranch were Thanksgiving and Christmas. Weddings were another source of celebration on the ranch. They were usually a community event; oftentimes the bride wore her Sunday best. Anniversary parties were similar to weddings, with the missus often wearing the same dress she was married in, though sometimes it had to be altered a wee bit.

Thanksgiving was celebrated by all. According to the Omaha, Nebraska, *World-Herald*, the cowboy looked forward to Thanksgiving not just because the fall roundup was likely over, but because of the variety of food. After being on the trail for months, cowboys and ranchers alike looked forward to the holiday. They reported, "In such an event all social restrictions are for the moment cast to the winds by the lordly cow king, who outdoes himself in hospitality towards his little army of rough riders. There is no 'second' table at the ranch that day, neither dining apart of the great man's household. But with mutual unity of design, employer and employees gather about the creaking digestive board, literally a sway with its weight of toothsome viands

. . . There is something positively unique about the cowboy Thanksgiving banquet—a refreshing absence of all restrains that elevates his feast above those which otherwise might be classed by contemporaries." Restaurants and homes alike had turkey, goose, cranberry sauce, pies, and all the trimmings similar to today. Of course, if the fall roundup wasn't completed, then the cowboy may have been subject to dining on the usual fare.

Christmas was also a big deal on the frontier, but not like today. Christmas was a time when family and friends celebrated all the joys of the year. Ranchers, farmers, and cowboys could take a break from their duties—within reason. Church was a large part of the holiday. Many people did not have a tree in their own home, but the church or community gathering place often did. Choirs sang, and presents were handed out. Food and more music followed.

The recipes and stories in this section capture those jubilant events.

Weddings on the Frontier

"We were soon engaged and we married at the old Bailey home on the T. & F. Ranch. A big dinner followed the ceremony and the festivities ended in a big square dance that night. Each friend took a piece of my wedding veil as a souvenir and my husband and I came to San Angelo the next day in grand style," recalled Mrs. Jack Miles of San Angelo, Texas.

Wedding ceremonies on the frontier varied from simple home services to lavish grand affairs.

Geography, social status, religion, and cash flow often dictated which type of wedding was held. Many western weddings were simple affairs—sometimes with meals and sometimes without. Often couples were married in the bride's parents' home and received gifts, then left for their honeymoon or their new home. Gifts ranged from money to tangible items like blankets, crockery, dishes, furniture, and livestock.

The menu items were as varied as the services and parties themselves. The *Fort Worth Daily Gazette* suggested these items for an October wedding in 1887: ham, turkey, scalloped oysters, shrimp and chicken salad, hot rolls, pickles, olives, cheese, caramel, angel food, figs, ice cream cakes, and foreign and domestic fruits.

CHICKEN SALAD

SERVES 2

    2 cups cooked chicken, cut or torn into
       bite-size pieces
    ½ cup diced celery
    ¼–½ cup homemade mayonnaise (See recipe
       this page.)
    Lettuce leaves
    Capers for garnish, optional

Combine the chicken, celery, and mayonnaise in a bowl.

Place a scoop of the chicken salad on a lettuce leaf and garnish with a few capers.

MAYONNAISE

MAKES ABOUT 2 CUPS

    1 hard-boiled egg yolk
    1 raw egg yolk
    ½ teaspoon salt
    Dash of cayenne pepper
    2 teaspoons apple cider vinegar
    ½ teaspoon yellow mustard
    1½ teaspoons lemon juice
    2 cups oil

Combine the egg yolks in a bowl and whip well.

Add the salt, pepper, vinegar, mustard, and lemon juice.

Slowly add the oil, drop by drop, while whipping the entire time.

Do this until the oil is gone and you have a smooth, creamy mayonnaise.

Variation: You can substitute commercial mayonnaise for the homemade, but add the mustard and taste the salad for seasoning. Adjust with salt and cayenne pepper.

RECIPES ADAPTED TEXAS'S *FREDERICKSBURG HOME KITCHEN COOK BOOK*, 1916.

ANGEL FOOD CAKE

MAKES 1 CAKE

> 1½ cups powdered sugar
> 1 cup sifted flour
> 1 teaspoon cream of tartar
> 12 eggs
> 1 teaspoon vanilla extract

Sift sugar, flour, and cream of tartar 4 times.

Separate the eggs and allow the whites to sit at room temperature for 30 minutes. Store the yolks for another use.

Beat the egg whites and vanilla extract in a large bowl with an electric mixer until peaks form.

Add the flour mixture in quarter batches to the egg whites and gently fold them until incorporated.

Pour into an ungreased angel-food-cake pan (tube pan) and gently cut through batter to remove any large air pockets.

Bake on the lowest rack at 350°F for 25–30 minutes or until top springs back when lightly touched.

Immediately invert cake (leave in pan) and allow to cool completely.

Loosen sides of cake from pan; remove cake.

RECIPE ADAPTED FROM KANSAS'S *PERRY HOME COOK BOOK*, 1920.

SHRIMP SALAD

SERVES 2–4

> 4 medium potatoes
> 1 cup cooked shrimp
> 3 hard-boiled eggs
> 1 bell pepper
> 4 sweet pickles, diced
> 1 cup mayonnaise
> Salt and pepper to taste

Peel, dice, and boil potatoes until tender, about 15 minutes.

Chop the shrimp, eggs, and pepper into bite-size pieces. Add the pickles.

Add the mayonnaise, salt, and pepper to taste.

RECIPE ADAPTED FROM KANSAS'S *PERRY HOME COOK BOOK*, 1920.

ICE CREAM CAKE

Even though the pioneers called this an ice cream cake, there is no ice cream in it all!

MAKES 1 CAKE

⅔ cup butter
2 cups sugar
1 teaspoon vanilla
6 egg whites, beaten
2½ cups flour
2 level teaspoons baking powder
1 cup milk

In a large bowl combine the butter and sugar and whip until light and fluffy.

Add the vanilla.

Beat the egg whites using an electric mixer until stiff peaks form; set aside.

Combine the flour and baking powder in a small bowl. Beginning and ending with flour, alternately add it and the milk to the butter and sugar, beating until mixed.

Gently fold in the egg whites and turn until combined.

Pour into a greased 11 x 14-inch pan and bake at 350°F for 30–35 minutes or until done. Check with a toothpick.

Frost with fluffy icing. (See recipe this page.)

FLUFFY ICING

FROSTS 1 CAKE

2 cups sugar
2 teaspoons lemon juice
⅔ cup water
3 egg whites
Candied violets, optional

Place the sugar, lemon juice, and water into a medium saucepan and bring to a boil. Boil and do not stir. It should be thick and bubbly and should look like thread if spun from a spoon; 10–15 minutes. Liquid will be reduced by half.

Beat egg whites in a large bowl.

When the sugar is ready gradually add it to the egg whites while beating. Whip with a mixer constantly until stiff peaks form, 5–7 minutes. Allow to cool to room temperature.

Frost cake and decorate with candied violets.

RECIPES ADAPTED FROM ST. LOUIS, MISSOURI'S *REPUBLIC*, MAY 27, 1900.

Thanksgiving on the Frontier

A Roar from the Bunkhouse

Nary a thing to eat Thanksgivin'
 Only tin can truck!
Gettin' tired of such a livin',
 Blame the orn'ry luck!
Nothin' only beans an' bacon—
Pard, excuse these tears!
Seems jest like we've been fursaken—
Darn this punchin' steers!
Folks back home are jest a-stuffin'
 Turkey-meat an' pie;
At them feed-fests there's no bluffin';
 Gosh, it makes me sigh!
No sich dinner for us fellers
 In this camp appears;
Turkey ain't fer cowboys' smellers—
Darn this punchin' steers!
Weather soggy-like an' murky;
 Makes me mighty blue;
Thinkin' of Thanksgivin' turkey
 Makes me h'umsick, too.

Sour-dough bread an' canned tomaters
 Ain't th' grub that cheers;
Oh fer pie an' mashed pertaters!
 Darn this punchin' steers!
Bunkhouse bunch are sick as blazes
 Bein' fed this way;
Gettin' so th' maynoo raises
Sam Hill ev'ry day!
ev'ry mother's son a-kickin'
When th' truck appears!
Never git a sniff o' chicken—
Darn this punchin' steers!
Same ol' bread an' beans furever!
Gosh, we'd like a change!
Reck'n we won't git it never
 While we ride th' range!
Oh, fer some o' mother's cookin;—
That's th' dope that cheers!
Guess my callin' I've mistooken—
DARN this punchin' steers!

—E. A. Brininstool, *Trail Dust of a Maverick*, 1914

People have been giving thanks since the Pilgrims' first harvest, and western pioneers began making this a big celebration shortly after Lincoln announced the holiday in 1863. That same year newspapers all over the West contained ads for balls, suppers, and other celebratory events. What you ate for your meal depended upon where you lived.

Menu items from ranches, bunkhouses, and local restaurants included many of the traditional favorites we still enjoy today, like turkey; cranberry sauce; and mince, apple, and pumpkin pies.

The hotels and restaurants in Helena, Montana, outdid themselves for Thanksgiving; cowboys and ranchers living near Helena, Montana, had much to choose from.

Manager Walker of the Hotel Helena offered an extensive bill of fare that he served from 6 to 8 p.m.

Blue Points (Oysters)

Soup: Potage a la Princesso and Consommé a la Royale

Fish: Boiled Red Snapper with Sauce Genoise served with Potatoes Duchesse, Lettuce, Celery, and Quince Olives

Boiled: Buffalo Tongue with Sauce Piquant

Entrees: Fried Chicken a la Anglaise, Croquettes of Pheasant a la Italienne, Salmi of Wild Goose a la Francaise, and Peach Charlotte Meringue with Rum Sauce

Roast: Turkey with Dressing and Cranberry Sauce, Ribs of Beef au Jus, Venison with Jelly Sauce, and Victoria Punch

Game: Broiled Quail on Toast and Opossum stuffed with Sweet Potatoes

Cold: Boiled Ham, Head Cheese, Chicken Salad, and Tomato Salad

Vegetables: New Potatoes in Cream, Mashed Potatoes, Baked Sweet Potatoes, Asparagus on Toast with Sauce Hollandaise, Cauliflower with Butter Sauce, and French Peas

Pastry: Mince Pie, Pumpkin Pie, English Plum Pudding with Hard and Brandy Sauce, Assorted Cakes, Chartreuse Jelly, Charlotte Russe, Tutti Frutti Ice Cream, Nuts, Figs, Raisins, Fruit, Bent's Wafer Crackers, Roquefort and Edam Cheese, and Coffee

CRANBERRY SAUCE

SERVES 4–6

- 1 quart cranberries
- 1 pint water
- 1 pound sugar

Place the cranberries in a large saucepan and cover with water.

Cover the saucepan with a lid and simmer until the berries split.

Add the sugar and allow to gently boil for about 20 minutes.

Place in a container and chill until ready to serve.

RECIPE ADAPTED FROM THE OMAHA, NEBRASKA, *WORLD-HERALD*, FEBRUARY 20, 1890.

STUFFED TURKEY

SERVES 10–14

- 1 (16–20-pound) turkey
- Dressing (See recipe on facing page.)
- Flour
- 4 tablespoons butter or margarine, softened
- Salt and pepper to taste

Remove the excess fat from the cavity of the turkey and discard.

Remove the giblets and neck and place in the roasting pan to flavor the pan juices.

Rinse and dry the turkey inside and out.

Stuff the cavity and the neck area with the dressing.

Once stuffed, truss the neck area, then the cavity. Be sure to tie the legs as well.

Rub the bird with flour and then with butter or margarine. Sprinkle with salt and pepper.

Cover and bake at 350°F. Be sure to baste the bird every 30–40 minutes, until done.

To obtain a golden color, remove the lid 30 minutes before cooking time is up. A bird this size should take approximately 3½–4 hours to cook.

You can stick a fork in the inside leg area to see if the juices run clear; once they do, the turkey is done.

DRESSING

MAKES ENOUGH TO STUFF 1 VERY LARGE TURKEY

4 ounces (1 stick) butter, cut up
8 ounces bread crumbs
2 tablespoons chopped parsley
2 teaspoons each thyme and marjoram
1 tablespoon grated lemon peel
Juice of ½ lemon
½ teaspoon nutmeg
1 teaspoon salt
Pepper to taste
2 eggs, beaten

Mix all the ingredients in a bowl.

RECIPES ADAPTED FROM THE *KANSAS CITY TIMES*, NOVEMBER 20, 1887.

TOMATO SALAD

SERVES 4–6

4–6 large ripe tomatoes
½ cup chopped cabbage
½ cup chopped celery
Salt and pepper to taste

Place tomatoes in a bowl that will not break from hot water. Pour boiling water over them and then peel each tomato. Discard liquid.

Cut the tomatoes into small pieces and add cabbage and celery.

Add salt and pepper and toss with salad dressing (See recipe on this page.)

SALAD DRESSING

MAKES ½ CUP

4 hard-boiled egg yolks
¼ cup oil
1 tablespoon mustard
1 teaspoon salt
½ teaspoon pepper
2 teaspoons sugar
1 teaspoon Worcestershire sauce
1 teaspoon white vinegar

Mash the egg yolks in a bowl and add the remaining ingredients.

Blend until there are no lumps.

Taste for seasoning and add more salt and pepper if needed.

Chill until ready to use.

RECIPES ADAPTED FROM THE *WYOMING COMMONWEALTH*, OCTOBER 3, 1891.

giving this year, and propose that their
many friends shall join with them. It will
be seen on the menu which follows that the
dinner at the Grand Central to-day will be
equal to any served in this section of the
country. That it will be well patronized
goes without saying, as the guests of the
house know they will receive the best in the
market. Dinner will be served from 12 to
two p. m.

New York Counts.

Green Sea Turtle.   Chicken Consomme.

Queen Olives.

Baked Red Snapper, a la Maitre d'Hotel.
Potatoes a la Windsor.

Dressed Lettuce.

Boiled Chicken, Oyster Sauce.
Green Peas.

Mayonaisse of Celery.

Fillet of Beef Pique, a la Montglas.
Croquettes of Sweetbreads. Bearnaise.
Chatreuse of Orange. Whipped Cream.

Roman Punch.

Roast Young Turkey Stuffed, Cranberry Sauce.
Browned Potatoes.

Prime Ribs of Beef, Demi Glace.
Sugar Corn.

Domestic Duck, Apple Sauce.
Lima Beans.

California Celery.

Haunch of Antelope, Pineapple Marmalade.
Stewed Tomatoes.

Cold Boned Turkey.   Goose Liver in Aspic.

Thanksgiving Pudding, Liquor Sauce.

Green Apple Pie.   Pineapple Cream Pie.

Mince Pie.

New York Vanilla Ice Cream. Port Wine Jelly.

Paris Rolls.   English Fruit Cake.

Macaroons.   Kisses.   Lady Fingers.

Mixed Nuts.   French Bon-Bons.

Delaware Grapes.   Baldwin Apples.

American Cheese.   Bent's Water Crackers.

Coffee Noir.

The Grand Central Hotel in Helena,
Montana, advertised a large spread to
entice diners for Thanksgiving dinner.
This menu was published in the *Daily
Independent*, November 26, 1891.

About 130 miles northeast of Helena was Fort Benton, which served as a fur-trading outpost. Prominent Montana merchant and cattleman John T. Murphy called the area of Fort Benton home. He founded the Powder River Land and Cattle Company and the Montana Cattle Company, also known as the Seventy-Nine Ranch.

The Choteau was a popular hotel in Fort Benton and offered up a traditional Thanksgiving menu.

Soup: Mock Turtle and Chicken

Fish: Booth's Raw Oysters and Baked Fresh Salmon with Tomato Sauce

Boiled: Corned Beef, Leg of Mutton with Caper Sauce, Sugar-cured Bacon with Cabbage, Ox Heart with Oyster Salad

Roast: Turkey with Cranberry Sauce, Spring Chicken with Sage Dressing, Sirloin of Beef, Loin of Pork with Applesauce, Loin of Mutton, Boss Ribs of Buffalo with Jelly

Entrees: Fresh Oyster Patties, Chicken Fricassee, Fillet de Beouf aux Truffles, Giblet Pie, Salmi of Prairie Chicken, and Dates de Foie Gras

Cold: Pressed, Spiced Corned Beef, Buffalo Tongue, Baked Sugar-cured Ham, and Chicken Salad

Relishes: Worcestershire Sauce, Young American Cheese, Stuffed Mangoes, Sweet Pickles, and Celery

Pastry: Cranberry Pie, Mince Pie, Lemon Pie, and English Plum Pudding with Brandy Sauce

Dessert: Wine and Brandy Jellies, Pound Cake, Lady Fingers, Jelly Cake, Fruits, Nuts, Raisins, Tea and Coffee

LOIN OF PORK WITH APPLESAUCE

SERVES 4–6

1 (3–4 pound) boneless pork roast
½ teaspoon salt
¼ teaspoon freshly ground pepper
¼ cup flour
Applesauce

Sprinkle the roast with the salt and pepper.

Roll it around in the flour.

Place the pork in a roasting pan, fat side up.

Bake uncovered for 2–2½ hours at 325°F. A meat thermometer should register 170°F when the roast is done.

Allow to stand for 15 minutes before slicing.

Serve with applesauce (see recipe in chapter 3).

RECIPE ADAPTED FROM *SCAMMELL'S CYCLOPEDIA OF VALUABLE RECEIPTS*, 1897.

CHICKEN SOUP

MAKES ABOUT 5 CUPS

1 (3–4 pound) chicken, quartered
2–3 quarts water
1 cup chopped celery
1 onion, chopped
1 tablespoon butter
1 tablespoon flour
1 tablespoon chopped Italian parsley
½ teaspoon salt
¼ teaspoon freshly ground pepper

Boil water, chicken, celery, and onion in a large stockpot for about an hour, or until the chicken is tender.

Skim off the top of the stock. Remove and debone the chicken and set aside.

Strain and measure 5 cups of the stock; set aside.

In the same stockpot, melt the butter and add the flour to make a roux.

Cook over medium heat for about 3 minutes.

Whisking constantly, slowly stir in the chicken stock.

Add the chicken, parsley, salt, and pepper and check the seasoning. Simmer for 5 minutes.

RECIPE ADAPTED FROM THE *DALLAS MORNING NEWS*, NOVEMBER 22, 1891.

CRANBERRY PIE

MAKES 1 PIE

> 2 cups fresh cranberries
> 1 cup sugar
> ¼ cup flour
> ¼ cup water or orange juice
> 2 piecrusts

Combine the berries in a bowl and add sugar, flour, and water or juice.

Pour into a piecrust and cover with the second piecrust.

Pinch together and bake at 350°F for 35–40 minutes or until bubbly.

Serve warm or cold.

RECIPE ADAPTED FROM *SCAMMELL'S CYCLOPEDIA OF VALUABLE RECEIPTS*, 1897.

Christmas

Christmas, whether on the ranch, in town, or on the trail, was at the very least recognized. Many attended church, offered prayers and thanks, opened presents, and enjoyed delicious viands. Even those in remote locations recognized the day with a meal or a small offering to a friend. A simple peel from an orange to scent a drawer or a piece of candy was often a cherished gift.

A Christmas tree in every home was not common until the late 1800s and early 1900s. People who did have their own trees tended to decorate them on Christmas Eve. Those who did not would enjoy their town's or church's tree. Santa and gifts were generally reserved for Christmas Eve, while Christmas Day was spent in church and feasting.

Charles Siringo was a cowboy who worked in Texas and New Mexico and later wrote about his life. He also claims to have been associated with some notable western characters, including Pat Garrett, Billy the Kid, and Clay Allison. He remembered Christmas in New Mexico while looking for Pat Garrett: "One Christmas Eve, Ash (Upson) and I put up for the night at the Jones ranch on Seven Rivers. Mr. and Mrs. Jones were warm friends of Mr. Upson's—hence they invited us to lay over Christmas and eat turkey dinner with them, which we did. We 'shore' enjoyed the turkey, sweet-potatoes, pumpkin pie and egg-nog."

PUMPKIN PIE

MAKES 1 PIE

- 2 cups pumpkin
- 1 teaspoon cinnamon
- ¾ cup honey
- ½ teaspoon freshly grated nutmeg
- ½ teaspoon salt
- 3 eggs, beaten
- 1 cup evaporated milk
- 1 single piecrust, unbaked

In a large bowl, combine all the ingredients except for the milk and piecrust.

Mix well and stir in the milk. Continue stirring until completely blended.

Pour into a 9-inch pie shell and bake at 375°F for 45–50 minutes. The pie is done when a knife inserted comes out clean.

Cool slightly before cutting.

RECIPE ADAPTED FROM THE *FREDERICKSBURG* (TEXAS) *HOME KITCHEN COOK BOOK*, 1916.

Pumpkin pie was and still is a traditional holiday favorite

SWEET POTATOES, MASHED

SERVES 4–6

 2 cups mashed sweet potatoes
 ¼ cup molasses
 1 egg, beaten
 1 cup brown sugar
 2 teaspoons ground ginger
 1 teaspoon cinnamon
 ½ teaspoon ground cloves
 ½ teaspoon orange peel
 ½ teaspoon grated nutmeg
 ¼ teaspoon salt
 Brown sugar for topping

Combine all the ingredients in a large bowl and mix until blended.

Butter a baking dish and pour mixture into it.

Sprinkle some sugar on top and bake at 350°F for about 25 minutes or until golden on top.

RECIPE ADAPTED FROM THE *DENVER EVENING POST*, JANUARY 31, 1896.

EGGNOG

MAKES 2–3 SERVINGS

 3 eggs, separated
 1 cup plus 1 tablespoon powdered sugar,
  divided
 1½ cups cream
 ¼ teaspoon nutmeg
 ¼ cup rum flavoring
 Grated cinnamon and nutmeg for garnish

Beat the egg yolks and 1 cup sugar together in a bowl and set aside.

Beat the egg whites with 1 tablespoon sugar until stiff peaks form, and refrigerate.

Heat the cream and nutmeg in a medium saucepan over medium-high heat and bring just to a boil, stirring occasionally.

Remove from the heat and gradually add hot cream into the egg yolk and sugar mixture.

Return everything to the pan and cook until the mixture reaches 160°F. **Caution:** It's dangerous to consume raw eggs, so be sure to cook the yolks to 160°F. Remove from the heat and place in a bowl; set in the refrigerator to chill.

Add the rum flavoring, fold the egg whites into the egg-yolk mixture, and blend well. Serve with grated cinnamon and nutmeg.

RECIPE ADAPTED FROM THE *IDAHO DAILY STATESMAN*, DECEMBER 12, 1892.

This traditional nog was served during Christmas and New Year's during the nineteenth century.

A Tenderfoot Bride

We met Ohio natives Clarice and Jarvis Richards in chapter 3. Clarice wrote in *A Tenderfoot Bride: Tales from an Old Ranch*, as the character "Mrs. Brook," that Christmas on the ranch was quite different than in Ohio, but she didn't let that stop her from enjoying the holiday. She wrote, "Within a radius of many miles there were only three small children, and about them our Christmas festivities revolved. They furnished the excuse for the tree, but no work was too pressing, no snow too deep to prevent the boys from bringing the Christmas tree and greens from a small clump of pines which stood on top of a distant hill, like a dark green island in the midst of the prairie sea. Early on Christmas morning Steve started out with gaily bedecked baskets for the Mexicans, and at the ranch the greatest excitement prevailed. I dashed frantically between the bunkhouse and our kitchen to be certain that nothing was forgotten. The big turkeys were stuffed to the point of bursting, all the 'trimmings' were in readiness, and the last savory mince pies were in the ovens."

She also observed, "The boys spent most of the morning 'slicking up' and put on their red neckties, the outward and visible sign of some important event, then passed the remaining hours sitting around anxiously awaiting the arrival of the guests of honor and—dinner. Christmas was our one great annual celebration, a day of cheer and happiness, in which everyone joyously shared. It was a new experience in the life of the undomesticated cowpuncher, but he took as much satisfaction in the fact that 'Our tree was a whole lot prettier than the one I've saw in town' as though he had won a roping contest."

MINCE PIE

MAKES 1 PIE

  2½ cups mincemeat filling
    (See recipe this page.)
  2 piecrusts, unbaked

Line a 9-inch pie pan with 1 piecrust and fill
with the mincemeat mixture.

Cover with the second piecrust.

Pinch the dough together and flute the edges.

Bake at 400°F for 35–40 minutes, or until golden
brown.

Serve hot.

MINCEMEAT FILLING

MAKES ABOUT 4 QUARTS

  1½ pounds lean beef, cubed
  ¼ pound lard or shortening
  3 pounds tart apples, peeled and cored
  1 pound brown sugar
  1 cup beef stock
  1 cup cider vinegar
  2½ pounds raisins
  1 cup molasses
  ¼ cup candied lemon peel
  1½ teaspoons ground cloves
  1 tablespoon freshly grated nutmeg
  ½ teaspoon allspice
  1 tablespoon cinnamon
  1½ teaspoons salt

Put meat in a large pot, cover with water, and
simmer until tender.

Push the meat, lard or shortening, and apples
through a food chopper.

Place the chopped mixture back in the pot, add
remaining ingredients, and simmer for 1 hour,
stirring often.

The mixture can be canned or used immediately.

Note: You can make the pie without meat, just
skip the first 3 ingredients, chop the apples and
combine with the other ingredients and simmer
the remaining ingredients for an hour.

RECIPES ADAPTED FROM THE *KANSAS HOME COOK BOOK*, 1874.

Arizona Ranches and "Cowboys"

Herbert Hilsop, who ran the Empire Ranch in south-eastern Arizona with Walter Vail, was very proud of his first Christmas dinner at the ranch in 1876. He wrote to his sister Amy, "We spent Christmas as merry as we could . . . we sat down to a festive meal, which I had taken great trouble to cook and serve up as nicely and prettily as possible, not forgetting the familiar 'Wishing you a Merry Christmas' stuck in a stick at the top of the first successful plum-pudding at Empire Ranch, the inscription being in Spanish as well, so our sheepherder could see it [they had sheep on their ranch while they worked on acquiring the cattle] . . . I surrounded the pudding with brandy and set light to it in the regular old style. Though we are in a rough country we try to enjoy ourselves sometimes, not being able to get a wild turkey, we got four wild ducks . . . I trussed these as best I could and I thought equal to a poulterer, only I had no sage and onions but plenty of bread crumbs, salt, pepper, and butter, a beautiful dish of nice brown mashed potatoes which I ornamented to the best of my ability, along with plum-pudding and brandy-sauce, good coffee and two bottles of whiskey—the best we could get in the country."

He continued, "I could not procure all the articles necessary for the pudding, but substituted them as best I could. In the place of beef suet I had to use mutton fat and could not procure citron or lemons, but in the place of lemon I put an orange and chopped up the peel."

ROAST DUCK

SERVES 4–6

1 (4-pound) duck
1 teaspoon salt
½ teaspoon freshly ground pepper
½ cup butter
1 medium onion, diced
3 teaspoons dried sage
1½ cups bread crumbs
1 egg, beaten

Wash the duck and pat dry. Prick the duck all over with a fork.

Rub the duck with the salt and pepper.

Melt the butter in a saucepan over medium heat and add the onion. Sauté for about 10 minutes or until translucent.

Place in a bowl and add all remaining ingredients; stir to combine. Stuff the duck with this mixture and place it in an uncovered roasting pan and cook at 400°F for 15 minutes.

Reduce the heat to 350°F and bake for 2 hours or until desired doneness is reached. Allow to rest for 10 minutes and then slice and serve with currant or cranberry jelly.

RECIPE ADAPTED FROM *SCAMMELL'S CYCLOPEDIA OF VALUABLE RECEIPTS*, 1897.

ENGLISH PLUM PUDDING

Plum pudding doesn't contain plums at all. Prunes (dried plums) were originally used by Queen Elizabeth I, but since they were so costly, most people used raisins. Feel free to substitute some prunes for raisins or do a combination of the two. Beef or mutton suet (fat) was first used as a preserver so the pudding could be kept for months and be ready for Christmas.

MAKES 2 LARGE PUDDINGS

- 4 cups stale bread
- 4 cups milk
- 3 eggs, beaten
- ¾ cup butter, melted
- ½ cup sugar
- ½ cup molasses
- 1 teaspoon salt
- ¾ pound raisins, prunes, or a combination
- ½ teaspoon each cinnamon, cloves, and mace
- ¼ teaspoon nutmeg
- 1 teaspoon chopped orange peel
- Boiling water
- 1 cup fruit juice

Remove the crusts from the bread, cut or shred the bread into small pieces, and lay them on a baking sheet.

Bake at 300°F until dry—about 10 minutes, depending upon how dry the bread was to start.

Place the bread in a large bowl and cover with the milk. Let stand for about an hour or until the milk is absorbed and the bread is soft.

Beat the bread and milk until combined and then add the eggs, butter, sugar, molasses, salt, raisins, spices and orange peel.

Grease 2 (2-pound) coffee cans or 2 (2-quart) deep oven-proof dishes.

Fill each greased pan half full of batter. Cover with lids or heavy-duty aluminum foil.

Place the pudding containers in a large pot or roaster.

Pour boiling water one-third up the side of the cans and bake at 300°F for 2 hours. Test with a knife and if it comes out clean when put into center of a pudding, the pudding is done.

Pour juice over the puddings and allow to cool.

Refrigerate until ready to eat.

When ready to eat, heat in water bath like the one used for baking it, and pour more juice over it. The juice, however, will not flame as traditional pudding spirits would.

RECIPE ADAPTED FROM THE *KANSAS HOME COOK BOOK*, 1874.

She Was a Cowboy!

Arizonans received quite a surprise when a longtime "cowboy" revealed that he was a she. In 1899 Jack Hall was forced to reveal her true identity when she was arrested. The story was reported in an Arizona paper and, later, in the *San Francisco Call*. The headline read, "How Helen Jackson, Known as Jack Hall, Was Discovered after Leading a Cowboy's Life for Several Years."

The *Call* reported, "'Captain Dick Wells and Mrs. Wells, formerly Jack Hall, will leave next week for San Francisco en route for Portland, Or.' This is the item that heads the personal column of most of this week's Arizona papers. Back of this is a story that has set all Arizona agog. The tale of a woman masquerading in cowboy attire, lassoing cattle, taking part in shooting scrapes, and living the wild, free, adventurous life of the Arizona vaquero. The story of a woman, who, because her father had been hanged as a horse thief, changed her name, hid her sex and in the beating of hoof and the whizzing of bullets sought to drown the memory of the disgrace. As a fitting finale, when her sex was discovered, she married 'Captain Dick,' the bravest and boldest cowboy in all Arizona. It is a story linked with strange and dramatic incidents that could happen nowhere save in Arizona, where fact still puts fiction to blush and boot and spur have not altogether given way to patent leathers. It was just about a year ago that a slender, clean-shaven youth asked for work at one of the big cattle ranches near Williams. Captain Dick, who was the leader of the cowboys, engaged the 'tenderfoot,' and 'Jack Hall,' the name the applicant for work gave, won his spurs in the annual rodeo for which the cowboys were then preparing. By day Jack sat his horse rounding up the cattle and at night slept on the ground. He was quiet and distant toward the other cowboys, but for the most part they liked him. Before the first month had passed he had an opportunity to show his mettle.

"A number of cowboys were spending the night in a typical Arizona town—one saloon per every fifteen inhabitants. Jack Hall, in search of Captain Dick, dropped into one of the saloons. A cowboy, revolver in hand, was acting as master of ceremonies, while in the middle of the floor the barkeeper, half dead from fatigue, was doing a dance, to the amusement of the rest of the cowboys.

"When the barkeeper attempted to stop twirling his feet the cowboy shouted for more dancing and the master of ceremonies encouraged the barkeeper by popping his pistol bullets dangerously near his feet. Jack Hall watched the scene in silence until he saw that the barkeeper had reached the limit of his endurance. Then he deftly wrenched the pistol from the cowboy's hand and, turning it on him, said: 'If you want any more dancing, do it yourself.' The cowboy snatched another one, but Jack Hall was too quick for him. There was a quick, sharp report and a cry of pain. The cowboy was wounded in his right arm. Then Jack Hall did a strange thing. His were the fingers that bandaged his adversary's wounds. He attended to him, even cutting his food for him, until the cowboy was well. After that he was christened Nurse Jack and more often called simply 'Nurse.'

"He had an almost womanish way of caring for them if any fell ill. 'He ain't a drinker and he can't play cards worth a bill of frijoles, but he's all right dosing medicine and such things,' explained the cowboys. Moreover, he was all right when it came to handling a horse or revolver, which after all, counts more points in the cowboy's estimation than bottle or cards. Besides he had as a firm ally, Captain Dick, which in Arizona is the open sesame to any cowboy's friendship."

Captain Dick and Jack Hall rode together for a number of years and it's not known just when the Captain discovered Jack's identity. However Jack did nurse the Captain back to health when he was struck with typhoid fever. The two obviously spent a great deal of alone time together.

The story continued with how Jack's real identity was revealed: "It all came through the teacher in the country school asking Jack to ride into town to buy her some ribbon. It was late in the afternoon when Jack reached Williams (Arizona), the nearest town. He was in a hurry, and the startled customers in the dry-goods store hastily made way for a sun-brown, cowboy on a horse, who rode straight up to the goods-covered counter and demanded three yards of pink ribbon. It is perfectly proper for a cowboy to ride his horse into an Arizona saloon, but when it comes to a dry-goods store it is a questionable procedure. While the clerk was hastily measuring off the ribbon a lady customer came too close to the horse's hoofs and was knocked unconscious.

"The Constable and several deputies proved too many for Jack and he was straightway marched to jail. Captain Dick came to town as soon as heard of the affair. He called on 'Boy' at the jail, and to his surprise was shown to the woman's ward. 'Jack' had been forced to reveal her sex or be put in the men's quarters. During the three days before the trial Captain Dick became accustomed to 'Boy' in her new guise. She told him her story; how her father had been hanged, how her mother and little sisters had taken refuge with relatives in Portland and she herself had changed her name from Helen Jackson to Jack Hall and remained in Arizona to live the life of a cowboy.

"On the day of the trial the injured woman, having recovered from her blow, refused to prosecute. However, the Judge was called upon to use his official powers. In the crowded courtroom Captain Dick and 'Boy' were made husband and wife. The story was soon known all over the Territory. Not only the cowboys on that particular range but from far and wide the vaqueros have sent congratulations and gifts. 'Nurse Jack's' wedding gifts will always remind her of her year of cowboy life—riding whips, Mexican saddles and diver spurs, to say nothing of several pairs of splendid riding boots and a dozen sombreros. Captain Dick Wells is going to take his wife to Portland to visit her family; then they will return to the stirrup and Arizona, which means home to them. The cowboys have promised not to call her Mrs. Wells. She wants to be 'Nurse Jack' to them. And Captain Dick says she will always be 'Boy' to him."

From One Era to Another

The era of the cowboy came to a close as the end of the century neared. Ranches and cowboys still existed, but the need for the cattle drives was fading due to the railroad. The Quarter Circle V Bar ranch in Prescott, Arizona, found a way to keep the cowboy way of life alive.

In 1917 the ranch was selected as the filming site for the Lockwood Company's latest cowboy motion picture. Charles Hooker welcomed the stars, Miss Anna Little and Harold Lockwood, to the ranch, where they filmed for five days.

Prescott's *Weekly Miner* reported, "Harold Lockwood, Balshofer, and the others of the company have been congratulating themselves ever since on having secured the ideal leading woman for Lockwood's support in this Western drama, which is a story of life on a large cattle ranch in Arizona, and for which Miss Little's experience and ability is admirably suited. The leading woman is known as one of the best riders of the West, and in *Under Handicap* will be given an opportunity to display this as well as her acting talents. The Lockwood Company is at present ideally situated in camp on the ranch of one of the largest cattle owners in the State of Arizona. The players are quartered in a dozen tents, pitched by the banks of a winding stream, lined on both sides by walnut and Cottonwood trees, and surrounded by a thick growth of mesquite. The ranch house and barns are half a mile distant and between them and the motion picture headquarters is the camp of the rodeo, in which a hundred cowpunchers have just rounded up several thousand head of cattle, which are used in the picture. The Lockwood Company has its own chuck-wagon and cook, whose efforts are greeted three times daily with wild enthusiasm. The food supply is augmented by the guns of Balshofer, W. H. Bainbridge, and Charlie Stalling, who are all crack shots and are fortunately in a country abounding in game of all kinds. The 'old Days' of Western motion pictures are recapitulated every evening around campfire by Balshofer, Lockwood, James Youngdeer, Lester Cuneo, Bill Clifford, Anna Little, Spencer, and the cowpunchers who rode in the first pictures made in the West."

On the Range

Cowboy Andy Adams recalled his Christmas while he was working on the range in Wyoming. His Christmas treat was something cowboys called *bear sign*, which meant doughnuts. "Well, three days before Christmas, just when things were looking gloomiest, there drifted up from the Cheyenne country one of the old timers. He had been working out in the Panhandle country, New Mexico, and the devil knows where, since he had left that range. He had shown no signs of letting up at eleven o'clock the first night, when he happened to mention where he was the Christmas before. 'There was a little woman at the ranch,' said he, 'wife of the owner, and I was helping her get up dinner, as we had quite a number of folks at the ranch. She asked me to make the bear sign—doughnuts, she called them—and I did, though she had to show me how. Well, fellows, you ought to have seen them—just sweet enough, browned to a turn, and enough to last a week.'"

They were so impressed with this story that they made him stay on and make bear sign for their outfit through spring. Adams wrote, "After dinner our man threw off his overshirt, unbuttoned his red undershirt and turned it in until you could see the hair on his breast. Rolling up his sleeves, he flew at his job once more. He was getting his work reduced to a science by this time. He rolled his dough, cut his dough, and turned out the fine brown bear sign to the satisfaction of all."

A couple of days later, word had spread about their bear sign man in camp. Adams continued, "The next day was Christmas, but he had no respect for a holiday, and made up a large batch of dough before breakfast. It was a good thing he did, for early that morning 'Original' John Smith and four of his peelers rode in from the west, their horses all covered with frost. They must have started at daybreak—it was a good twenty-two mile ride. They wanted us to believe that they had simply come over to spend Christmas with us. Company that way, you can't say anything. But the easy manner in which they gravitated around that tub—not even waiting to be invited—told a different tale. They were not nearly satisfied by noon."

BEAR SIGN (DOUGHNUTS)

MAKES ABOUT 8 DOUGHNUTS

1¾ cups flour
½ teaspoon salt
2 teaspoons baking powder
½ teaspoon baking soda
¾ cup sugar
1 egg, beaten
½ cup buttermilk
1 tablespoon butter, melted
4 cups vegetable shortening or lard for frying

Sift the flour, salt, baking powder, and baking soda into a large bowl.

In a separate bowl, beat the egg and sugar until blended.

Add the milk to the egg and sugar and then the melted butter.

As you mix, the dough should become firm enough to roll. Do not overmix the dough or it will become tough.

Lightly dust the rolling surface with flour and roll out part of the dough into about ¼-inch thick.

Cut with a doughnut cutter or shape into doughnuts.

Heat the oil in a deep pot and add enough shortening so the doughnuts will float. The oil should be between 350° and 375°F.

Gently drop the doughnuts into the fat and allow to rise. Flip and cook for 1–2 minutes longer.

Remove to paper towels and allow to cool.

Frost with your favorite topping or dip into powdered or cinnamon sugar.

ICING

MAKES ENOUGH TO COMPLEMENT BEAR SIGN (DOUGHNUTS)

⅓ cup hot water
1 cup confectioner's sugar

Combine in bowl and dip the doughnuts in.

RECIPES ADAPTED FROM TEXAS'S *DENISON DAILY NEWS*, JANUARY 20, 1878.

In Town

Cattle prospects were good in New Mexico in 1885, and a glowing report about the fertile grasslands appeared in the *Las Vegas Gazette*. Down a few stories were menus from local hotels that served Christmas meals.

The Hot Springs Hotel offered:

Royal Select Oysters

Soup: Green Turtle, au Quenelles

Fish: Boiled Salmon with sauce Béarnaise or Baked Whitefish a la Chambord

Boiled: Turkey with Oyster Sauce and Leg of Southdown Mutton with Caper Sauce

Roast: Ribs of Christmas Beef, Stuffed Young Pig, Ham with glace champagne sauce, and Young Goose with Applesauce

Entrees: Filet of Beef Piquant a la Italienne, Croquettes of Chicken a la Tolouse, Calf's Sweetbreads with sauce a la St. Cloud, and Timbal of Macaroni a la Florentine

Cold Dishes: Boned Turkey with Jelly, Lobster Salad, Chicken Salad, and Pate de Foie Gras

Vegetables: Boiled Potatoes, Stewed Corn, Mashed Potatoes, Hubbard Squash, Green Peas, and Asparagus in Cream

Game: Saddle of Venison Hunter Style, Mallard Duck with Currant Jelly, and Partridge Larded with Petit Pois

Dessert: Apricot Pie, Cream Meringue Pie, Fruit Pudding with Brandy Sauce, Maraschino Jelly, Assorted Cake, Vanilla Ice Cream, Fruit, Coffee, and Nuts

BOILED SALMON WITH SAUCE BÉARNAISE

SERVES 4

   1–2 pounds wild caught salmon fillets
   ½ teaspoon salt
   1 bay leaf
   1 sprig fresh thyme
   1 slice onion
   ½ teaspoon peppercorns
   1 cup water
   1 slice lemon
   1 cup white wine vinegar

Bring all the ingredients to a simmer in a large skillet.

Cover and continue cooking for about 10 minutes.

The fish is done when a fork pierces it easily.

Remove fish from the pan and place on a serving platter.

Pour Béarnaise sauce (see recipe this page) over the salmon.

RECIPE ADAPTED FROM KANSAS CITY, KANSAS'S *THE TOPICS*, MAY 16, 1895.

BÉARNAISE SAUCE

MAKES ½ CUP

   4 tablespoons oil or clarified butter
   4 tablespoons white wine vinegar
   4 egg yolks
   ⅓ cup shallots, chopped
   3 sprigs fresh tarragon
   Salt and pepper to taste

Combine the oil, vinegar, and egg yolks and cook in a double boiler over low heat until thickened, about 2 minutes.

Remove from heat and add the shallots, tarragon, salt, and pepper.

Taste for seasoning.

RECIPE ADAPTED FROM THE *DALLAS MORNING NEWS*, SEPTEMBER 20, 1892.

LOBSTER SALAD

SERVES 4

> 2 cups cooked lobster meat
> ½ cup celery, chopped
> 4 hard-boiled egg yolks
> Salt and pepper to taste
> ½ cup white vinegar

Combine the lobster and celery in a mixing bowl.

In a small bowl, prepare the dressing: Mix the egg yolks, salt, pepper, and vinegar together until smooth.

Place lobster mixture on a platter and pour the dressing over.

RECIPE ADAPTED FROM THE *COLORADO COOK BOOK*, 1883.

APRICOT PIE

MAKES 1 PIE

> 1 pint apricots, canned or fresh, peeled, and
>   pitted
> ¾ cup juice
> ½ cup sugar
> 2 piecrusts, unbaked

Place apricots, juice, and sugar in a large saucepan.

Cook over medium heat for about 10 minutes or until a thick syrup forms.

Line a pie pan with 1 crust and pour in the apricots.

Cover with the second crust and bake at 400°F for 30 minutes or until crust is done.

RECIPE ADAPTED FROM WICHITA, KANSAS'S *THURSDAY AFTERNOON COOKING CLUB'S COOK BOOK*, 1922.

The Plaza Hotel's Christmas menu included:

Soup: Oxtail

Fish: Fried Mackinaw Trout with Oyster Sauce and Barataria Shrimp in Mayonnaise

Boiled: Capon with Celery Sauce and Tongue with Tomato Sauce

Roast: Sirloin of Beef, Turkey Stuffed with Oysters and served with Cranberry Sauce, and Leg of Mutton with Jelly

Entrees: Pineapple Fritters with Vanilla Flavoring, Fricassee of Lamb with French Peas, and Tenderloin of Beef Larded with Mushrooms

Vegetables: French Green Peas, Sugar Corn, Mashed and Browned Potatoes

Dessert: Mince Pie, Lemon Meringue Pie, English Plum Pudding with Brandy Sauce, Vanilla Ice Cream, Jelly Cake, Fruit Cake, White Mountain Cake, Jelly Roll, Nuts, Raisins, Assorted Fruit, Tea, French Drip Coffee, Iced Tea, and Cheese

TENDERLOIN OF BEEF, LARDED WITH MUSHROOMS

SERVES 4

1 (3 pound) beef fillet
1 pound mushrooms, cleaned and stemmed
1 teaspoon salt
½ teaspoon freshly ground pepper
¼ pound bacon

Preheat the oven to 400°F.

Place the beef in a roasting pan and add the mushrooms around it.

Sprinkle all with salt and pepper.

Place the bacon strips over the beef.

Put the roast in the oven and cook for 15 minutes at 400°F.

Reduce the heat to 350°F and cook for an additional 35–45 minutes.

For medium rare aim for an internal temperature of 135° or 145°F after removing from the oven.

For a medium roast, the internal temperature should be 150° or 160°F after standing.

Allow to rest 10 minutes before slicing.

Pour the mushrooms and the pan juices into a bowl and serve over the slices of beef.

RECIPE ADAPTED FROM WICHITA, KANSAS'S *THURSDAY AFTERNOON COOKING CLUB'S COOK BOOK*, 1922.

According to Webster's 1884 Dictionary, to *lard* something meant "to fatten or enrich or to mix with something by way of improvement."

BROWNED POTATOES

SERVES 4

> 10–12 small new potatoes, scrubbed
> ¼ cup butter, melted
> ½ teaspoon salt
> ¼ teaspoon freshly ground pepper

Place the potatoes in a baking dish and drizzle the butter over them.

Sprinkle with the salt and pepper.

Bake at 375°F for 20–30 minutes or until tender.

RECIPE ADAPTED FROM THE OMAHA, NEBRASKA, *SUNDAY WORLD-HERALD*, APRIL 23, 1899.

These potatoes are super easy to make and taste delicious.

JELLY CAKE

MAKES 1 CAKE

4 eggs (weigh them in their shells)
Butter, equal to the weight of the eggs;
   softened
Sugar, equal to the weight of the eggs
Flour, equal to the weight of the eggs
¼ teaspoon salt
Jelly, jam or marmalade, any kind

Cream the butter for about 5 minutes.

Add the sugar and beat for 2–3 minutes.

Add the eggs and beat for 3 minutes.

Add the flour and salt and beat for an additional 5 minutes.

Butter a 9 x 9-inch baking pan and pour in the batter.

Bake at 350°F for 20–25 minutes. Use a toothpick to test for doneness.

Cool in pan for 10 minutes and then allow to cool completely on a cake rack.

Cut the cake in half (to create layers) and spread the jam over the bottom of the cake. Place the other half of the cake on top and gently press the pieces together.

Cut them into long finger pieces.

Pile them in crossbars on a glass dish and serve.

RECIPE ADAPTED FROM THE *KANSAS HOME COOK BOOK*, 1874.

Captain Lasher at the Depot Hotel offered his customers this menu for Christmas:

Relishes: Celery and Radishes

Soup: Clam Chowder, Coney Island Style

Fish: Boiled Mackinaw Trout with Shrimp Sauce

Entrees: Charlotte of Fruit and Chicken Pot Pie with Dumplings

Roast: Stuffed Turkey with Cranberry Sauce and Loin of Beef, au jus

Game: Saddle of Venison with Currant Jelly

Cold Dishes: Boned Capon with Rhine Wine Jelly

Vegetables: Mashed Potatoes, Green (fresh) Corn, Stewed Tomatoes, Lima Beans, and Green Peas

Dessert: Mince Pie, Apple Pie, English Plum Pudding with Brandy Sauce, and Vanilla Ice Cream

Cheese: Holland, Stilton, Apples, Oranges, Teas, and Coffee

LIMA BEANS

SERVES 4

4 cups water
1 teaspoon salt
4 cup fresh lima beans
¼ teaspoon freshly ground pepper
1 tablespoon butter

Boil the water in a medium dutch oven; add the salt and lima beans.

Reduce the heat to medium and cook for 25–30 minutes, or until the beans become tender.

Drain and toss with butter and pepper.

RECIPE ADAPTED FROM SOUTH DAKOTA'S *GRAND FORKS DAILY HERALD*, NOVEMBER 1, 1883.

CLAM CHOWDER, CONEY ISLAND STYLE

SERVES 4

- ¼ pound salt pork or bacon, diced
- ½ cup water crackers, crushed
- 6 cloves
- 6 allspice balls
- 1 bottle clam juice
- 1 onion, diced
- 4 medium potatoes, cubed
- 2 cups chopped canned tomatoes
- 1 teaspoon salt
- ½ teaspoon freshly ground black pepper
- 2 cans clams, chopped
- 1 teaspoon Worcestershire sauce

Sauté pork fat or bacon over low heat in a medium stockpot and cook until browned. Place the crackers in a glass measuring cup and add enough boiling water to cover and let stand for 3 minutes. Drain off any excess water.

Tie the cloves and allspice together in gauze and add them with the clam juice, onions, potatoes, tomatoes, crackers, salt, and pepper to the salt pork or bacon.

Cook over low heat, uncovered for about 2 hours.

Add the clams and Worcestershire and cook another 5 minutes.

RECIPE ADAPTED FROM THE OMAHA, NEBRASKA, *WORLD-HERALD*, SEPTEMBER 10, 1893.

Christmas Cows

Cowboys from the ranches in Helena, Montana, including those from the N Bar Ranch, may have dined in downtown Helena on Christmas day at the Belvedere House. The N Bar Ranch dates back to 1878 when the Newman brothers brought their Nebraska cattle, which totaled twelve thousand, to Montana with a contract in hand to provide meat for the Indian reservations. Around 1886 an Irish immigrant named Tom Cruse bought the Newman's remaining herd and the N Bar brand.

Duncan McDonald offered this vast menu to his patrons from noon to three on Christmas day:

Soup: Cream Fowl and Consommé Melo of French Peas, Celery, Chow Chow, Tomato Catsup, and Oyster Pauloo

Fish: Braised Flounder with Olive Sauce, Boiled Trout, and Whitefish with Potato Croquettes

Boiled: Calf's Tongue with Macaroni, and Sugar Cured Ham with Champagne Sauce

Roast: Turkey with Cranberry Sauce, Pam Ribs, Young Pig with Oyster Dressing and Baked with Apple, 'Possum with Sweet Potato, and Venison with Lemon Jelly

Entrees: Sweetbread Croquettes with French Peas, Braised Pheasant Hunter Style, Fillet of Veal with Mushroom Sauce, Pigeon with Rice, and Cream Fritters with Banana Sauce

Vegetables: Mashed Potatoes, Brown Potatoes, Sweet Potatoes, Sugar Corn, and Tomatoes

Salads: Chicken Salad, Shrimp Salad, Cold Slaw, and Lobster

Cold Meats: Boned Pigeon with Madeira Dressing, Hog's Head Cheese, and Deviled Ham

Pastry: Mince Pie, Lemon Pie, Steam Pudding with Brandy Sauce, Orange Gelatine, Pineapple Ice Cream, and White Raisin Pudding with Somelee Sauce

Cakes: Fruit Cake, Coconut Cake, Ladies' Fingers, and Jelly Cake

Fruits: Oranges, Grapes, Bananas, Apples, and Mixed Nuts

Bread: Graham, Boston Brown, White, Soda Crackers, and Sweet Crackers

VENISON STEAK WITH LEMON JELLY

SERVES 2–4

    1 (2–3-pound) venison steak, 2 inches thick
Salt and pepper to taste
5 tablespoons butter, melted
Lemon Jelly (See recipe this page.)

Sauté the steak in a large frying pan over medium heat, turning the meat frequently so it doesn't brown. It should be medium-rare.

Season with salt and pepper to taste.

Allow to rest for 10 minutes, then slice and serve with the melted butter and lemon jelly.

RECIPE ADAPTED FROM ST. LOUIS, MISSOURI'S *THE REPUBLIC*, NOVEMBER 24, 1889.

LEMON JELLY

SERVES 4–6

    1 egg
1 cup sugar
1 teaspoon cornstarch
1 teaspoon butter
Juice of 1 lemon
2 cups boiling water

Beat the egg, sugar, cornstarch, and butter together.

Place in a saucepan and stir in the lemon juice and water.

Bring to a boil and stir constantly for about 3 minutes.

Allow to cool completely and serve. Refrigerate any remaining jelly.

RECIPE ADAPTED FROM THE *IDAHO AVALANCHE*, JULY 26, 1879.

TOMATO CATSUP

MAKES 1½ CUPS

- 2½ cups tomatoes, fresh-cooked or canned
- 1 teaspoon salt
- ½ teaspoon whole peppercorns, bruised
- 3 teaspoon pepper flakes
- ½ teaspoon cinnamon sticks
- ¼ teaspoon mace*
- ¾ teaspoon mustard seeds
- ½ teaspoon whole allspice
- 3 garlic cloves, peeled and sliced
- ¼ teaspoon cider vinegar (optional)

Note: You can substitute a piece of nutmeg for the mace.

Either cook fresh tomatoes to yield 2½ cups or use canned.

Place the tomatoes and salt in a saucepan and blend with an immersion blender, or use a standard blender and then pour the mixture into a saucepan.

Put the remainder of the spices in a piece of cheesecloth and tie. If using vinegar, add now.

Bring tomatoes and salt to a boil and then add the spice bag.

Cook over low heat for 1–3 hours for your desired thickness.

Remove from the heat and take out the spice bag.

Condiments like ketchup, mustard, and mayonnaise were made from scratch and were not commercially prepared until the early twentieth century.

Put into a storage container and refrigerate.

Note: The original recipe says this will keep for 20 years if corked properly!

RECIPE ADAPTED FROM *THE DAILY BULLETIN SUPPLEMENT*, SAN FRANCISCO, CALIFORNIA, SEPTEMBER 23, 1876.

POTATO CROQUETTES

SERVES 4–6

4 medium potatoes, peeled and boiled
1 ounce butter
Pinch each of salt, nutmeg, and sugar
1 egg
3 eggs, beaten in a separate bowl
Bread crumbs
½ cup oil and ½ cup butter, combined for
     frying
Salt for sprinkling

Mash the potatoes and add the butter, salt, nutmeg, sugar, and 1 egg.

Mix well, but do not overbeat.

Chill for 1 hour.

When cool, shape into cylinders or balls and then dip in beaten eggs.

Next, dip in bread crumbs.

Melt the oil and butter in a deep cook pot over medium-high heat.

Gently place the croquettes into the oil and fry until golden.

Drain on a paper towel and season with salt.

RECIPE ADAPTED FROM ST. LOUIS, MISSOURI'S *THE REPUBLIC*, MARCH 23, 1896.

Croquettes were a frugal way of turning leftovers into a meal.

COCONUT CAKE

MAKES 1 CAKE

1 cup butter
2 cups sugar
4 eggs
1 teaspoon vanilla or lemon extract
3 cups flour
2 teaspoon baking powder
¼ teaspoon salt
1 cup milk
1–2 cups shredded coconut

Cream butter and sugar together in a large bowl.

Add the eggs and vanilla and beat until smooth and foamy.

Combine the flour, baking powder, and salt in a small bowl and stir.

Alternately add the flour and milk to the egg mixture; beginning and ending with the flour.

Once combined, beat for about 3 minutes until light and fluffy.

Pour into greased and floured 9-inch cake pans.

Bake at 350°F for 30–35 minutes or until done. Test with a toothpick.

Cool in pans for 10 minutes and then turn onto cake racks to cool completely before frosting. Spread on your favorite frosting.

Cover the frosting with coconut to your liking.

RECIPE ADAPTED FROM THE *KANSAS HOME COOK BOOK*, 1874.

The Grand Fork, North Dakota's *Daily Herald* ran a story about Arizona cowboys during Christmas in 1887, observing that "one of the most comical features of ranch life is the absence of femininity. No wonder. We are two hundred miles from a milliner's shop, with the distance constantly on the increase. Last Christmas a desperate effort was made to celebrate the occasion with a ball. Over 10,000 square miles of territory was raked over, and the result was seven fair maidens and over forty dancing men. Each lady had six dancing partners—a rather more than Scripture allowance."

Coconut cake was a popular dessert in most Victorian homes and restaurants.

BIBLIOGRAPHY

Adams, Andy. *The Log of a Cowboy*. Cambridge, Mifflin & Co., 1903.

Adams, Ramon F. *Western Words: A Dictionary of the Range, Cow Camp, and Trail*. Oklahoma City, University of Oklahoma Press, 1945.

Bates, Frank A. *Camping and Camp Cooking*. Boston, The Ball Publishing Company, 1909.

Cleaveland, Agnes Morley. *No Life for a Lady*. New York, Houghton Mifflin, 1941

Fridge, Ike. *History of the Chisum War*. Electra, Smith Printers, Date unknown.

Gregory, Scott. *Sowbelly and Sourdough: Original Recipes from the Trail Drives and Cow Camps of the 1800s*. Caldwell, Caxton Press, 1995.

Henty, G. A. *Redskin and Cow-boy: A Tale of the Western Plains*. New York, Charles Scribner's Sons, 1894.

James, W. S. *Cowboy Life in Texas*. Chicago, M. A. Donohue, 1892.

Ladies of Leavenworth. *The Kansas Home Cook-Book: Consisting of Recipes Contributed by Ladies of Leavenworth and Other Cities and Towns*. Leavenworth, KS, 1874; Kansas City, MO, Andrews McMeel Publishing, 2013.

Library of Congress. *WPA Life Histories*. www.loc.gov/collections/federal-writers-project/.

Post, C. C., and Tex Bender. *Ten Years a Cowboy*. Chicago, Rhodes & McClure Publishing Co., 1898.

Roosevelt, Theodore. *Ranch Life and the Hunting Trail*. New York, The Century Company, 1896.

Scammel, Henry B. *Cyclopedia of Valueable Receipts*. St. Louis, Planet Publishing Co., 1897.

Siringo, Charles A. *A Lone Star Cowboy*. Santa Fe, 1919

———. *A Texas Cow Boy*. Chicago: Siringo & Dobson, 1886.

The Ladies Auxiliary. *The Fredericksburg Home Kitchen Cook Book*. Fredericksburg, TX, Ladies Auxiliary, 1916.

The Young Ladies Mission Band. *Colorado Cook Book*. Denver, Collier & Cleveland, 1883.

True West magazine. Cave Creek, Arizona.

Utley, Robert. *Encyclopedia of the American West*. San Antonio, Wings, 1997.

CONNECTIONS TO THE PAST

Arbuckles' Coffee, arbucklecoffee.com.
Oregon Trail Sourdough Starter (free), carlsfriends
    .net/source.html
Texas Ranch Life, texasranchlife.com

INDEX OF RECIPES BY TYPE

ABOUT THE AUTHOR

On the heels of her last cookbook, *Frontier Fare*, Sherry Monahan has culled stories and recipes from cattle trails, cow towns, cowboys, and cattle ranches. She has penned her Frontier Fare column since 2009 for *True West* magazine. She studied cooking in school and has a passion for all things food. She has a collection of over 150 cookbooks, with the oldest being from 1869.

Sherry is the author of several books on the Victorian West, including *Frontier Fare: Recipes and Lore from the Old West*; *Mrs. Earp: The Wives and Lovers of the Earp Brothers*; *California Vines, Wines & Pioneers*; *Taste of Tombstone: A Hearty Helping of History*; *Pikes Peak: Adventurers, Communities, and Lifestyles*; *The Wicked West: Boozers, Cruisers, Gamblers, and More*; and *Tombstone's Treasure: Silver Mines and Golden Saloons*. She is currently working on books about holidays on the frontier, pie, sourdough, and an English frontier family who lost more than just its money.

Sherry has appeared on *Legends and Lies*, hosted by Bill O'Reilly, on Fox News and on *Gunslingers* on the American Heroes Channel. She's also appeared on the History Channel in many shows, including *Cowboys & Outlaws: The Real Wyatt Earp*; *Lost Worlds: Sin City of the West* (Deadwood); *Investigating History*; and two of the *Wild West Tech* shows. She received a Wrangler at the Western Heritage Awards for her performance in *Cowboys & Outlaws* in 2010.

Larry Monahan

Sherry is president of Western Writers of America (2014–2016) and holds memberships in the following organizations: James Beard Foundation, Women Writing the West, the Authors Guild, Wild West History Association, Association of Professional Genealogists, and Westerners International. She is also a charter member of the National Women's History Museum.

Sherry is a marketing consultant, food stylist, and professional genealogist, and she also traces the genealogy of foods and wines. She calls it Winestry and says, "History never tasted so good!"

Visit her at sherrymonahan.com.